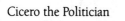

Cicero the Politician

Ancient Society and History

Cicero the

CHRISTIAN HABICHT

Politician

The Johns Hopkins University Press
Baltimore and London

This book has been brought to publication with the generous assistance
of the David M. Robinson Fund.

The Johns Hopkins University Press
701 West 40th Street
Baltimore, Maryland 21211
The Johns Hopkins Press Ltd., London

The paper used in this publication meets the minimum requirements of
American National Standard for Information Sciences—Permanence of
Paper for Printed Library Materials, ANSI Z39.48-1984.

Library of Congress Cataloging-in-Publication Data

Habicht, Christian.
    Cicero the politician / Christian Habicht.
        p.   cm.—(Ancient society and history)
    Bibliography: p.
    Includes index.
    ISBN 0-8018-3872-X (alk. paper)
    1. Cicero, Marcus Tullius—Political and social views. 2. Cicero,
Marcus Tullius—Contemporary Rome. 3. Rome—Politics and
government—265–30 B.C. 4. Authors, Latin—Biography.
5. Statesmen—Rome—Biography.   I. Title.   II. Series.
PA6320.H33   1990
937'.05'092—dc20   89-45485
                                                                 CIP

Contents

Preface

This book is a revised version of six lectures given in 1987 as the Louise Taft Semple Lectures at the University of Cincinnati and at the Johann Wolfgang Goethe - Universität, Frankfurt/Main. While it is my hope that specialists may not find it entirely without merit, its intended audience are primarily students of history and nonspecialists interested in the topic but not content to have only the author's word for it. Notes and bibliography have been added for their benefit, since I am convinced that there are readers, besides scholars, who would like to check on the state of affairs of certain matters for themselves. Books without annotation, such as Christian Meier's *Caesar* (1982) or Pierre Grimal's *Cicéron* (1986), do not allow for that.

On the political events of Cicero's time, not much can be said today that is both new and true. Matters are somewhat different for Cicero the politician himself. His image continues to suffer from harsh verdicts, despite the meritorious efforts to do him justice, begun over a century ago with Gaston Boissier's famous *Cicéron et ses amis* (Paris 1865, often reprinted). The need persists to strike a balance once again. In my attempt to do this, I do not intend to persuade anyone that Cicero was (or, without Caesar, could have been) a great politician, but simply to show that he was, body and soul, a politician. It hardly needs saying that his performance as such cannot be properly assessed without an appreciation of the conditions under which he and his contemporaries operated.

The narrative combines general background information and specific details. In choosing the material to be presented, I had to be selective, but I tried not to be partisan beyond the unavoidable. Translations from ancient authors are those of the Loeb Classical Library volumes (where they exist), except for Cicero's correspondence and *Philippics*, where Shackleton Bailey's translations have been used. The remaining translations from foreign languages, except where otherwise indicated, are my own.

It is a pleasure to express my sincere gratitude to the colleagues at the University of Cincinnati and Frankfurt for the invitation to lecture and for their hospitality. D. R. Shackleton Bailey and A. S. Bradford were kind enough to read an early draft, K. Bringmann, K. Clinton, and W. Eder a somewhat more advanced draft of the manuscript. Each saved me from a number of errors and infelicities, as did several anonymous referees. I am most grateful to all these colleagues. Julia Bernheim improved the English on every page; she and Sandra S. Lafferty prepared the typescript with exemplary care. Eric Halpern, Ann Waters, and Therese Boyd applied the same care in transforming it into a book. My warmest thanks go to all five.

Abbreviations

For ancient authors, see the *Oxford Classical Dictionary*, 2nd ed.,
pp. ix–xxii; for works cited in an abbreviated form, see the Bibliography.

Abh.Leipzig	*Abhandlungen der sächsischen Akademie, Leipzig*
AHR	*American Historical Review*
AJAH	*American Journal of Ancient History*
AJPh	*American Journal of Philology*
AnnPisa	*Annali della R. Scuola Normale Superiore di Pisa, Sezione di Lettere*
ANRW	*Aufstieg und Niedergang der römischen Welt*
Antcl	*L'antiquité classique*
A & R	*Atene e Roma*
CJ	*Classical Journal*
CP	*Classical Philology*

CQ	*Classical Quarterly*
CR	*Classical Review*
CW	*Classical World*
G & R	*Greece and Rome*
GRBS	*Greek, Roman and Byzantine Studies*
HSCP	*Harvard Studies in Classical Philology*
HZ	*Historische Zeitschrift*
JRS	*Journal of Roman Studies*
Kl.Schr.	*Kleine Schriften*
LCM	*Liverpool Classical Monthly*
MEFRA	*Mélanges d'archéologie et d'histoire de l'Ecole française de Rome*
MH	*Museum Helveticum*
NAG	*Nachrichten von der Göttinger Akademie der Wissenschaften*
PCPS	*Proceedings of the Cambridge Philological Society*
PP	*La Parola del Passato*
RAC	*Reallexikon für Antike und Christentum*
RE	A. Pauly and G. Wissowa, *Realencyclopädie der classischen Altertumswissenschaft, 1893–1978*
Rendic.Accad.Lincei	*Rendiconti della Accademia dei Lincei*
REA	*Revue des études anciennes*
REL	*Revue des études Latines*
Rev.phil.	*Revue de philologie, de littérature et d'histoire ancienne*

RhM	*Rheinisches Museum für Philologie*
Riv.FC	*Rivista di Filologia e d'Istruzione Classica*
Riv. stor. ant.	*Rivista storica dell' antichità*
Savigny-Zeitschr.	*Savigny-Zeitschrift für Rechtsgeschichte, Romanistische Abteilung*
StudClassOrient	*Studi classici e orientali*
SymbOsl	*Symbolae Osloenses*
TAPA	*Transactions and Proceedings of the American Philological Association*

Cicero the Politician

Chapter One

Cicero and the Late Republic

new book on Cicero needs some justification, since there is no shortage of books and papers on his life, personality, and achievements. Year after year, some hundred new items are added to an already incredibly rich and varied bibliography; even a play called *Cicero* by Sam Segal went on the New York stage in October 1986. Cicero's heritage is so rich and diversified that something new can always be said. The justification for yet another book could therefore be that coming to grips with him is always worth another serious effort. More important to the present topic, however, is this: while Cicero the man of letters is universally acclaimed, Ciero the politician is not; opinions on this score vary enormously, and Cicero still suffers, as he did during the nineteenth century, from malignant criticism.

For the ancient historian, the history of the late Republic is the ultimate challenge. The twenty years from 63 to 43 B.C., that is, the period from Cicero's consulate to his death, are by far the best-known years from all antiquity. And no one else in antiquity is as well known as Marcus Tullius Cicero, with Julius Caesar and the emperor Julian far behind. Our knowledge comes mainly, although not exclusively, from Cicero himself. It results from his productivity as a writer and his unfailing willingness to talk about himself, both publicly and in confidential letters. He delivered several hundred speeches; according to the latest count, no less than 163 are known by their titles (58 of which are extant).[1] Furthermore, a substantial fraction of his tremendous correspondence survives: more than 800 letters he wrote and 90 addressed to him (unfortunately not a single one by the shrewd, trusted, and discreet friend Atticus). Some of these letters have the length of a substantial essay. There are, finally, his books on rhetoric, philosophy, religion, and other related topics, some twenty-five titles, most of them extant.

From this and other evidence, the life of an important man can be traced in great detail for the last twenty years of his career, sometimes from day to day, even from hour to hour. During these years Cicero, as a former consul, was one of the "elder statesmen." These same years witnessed the rise and fall of Julius Caesar, the ruin of the Roman Republic, and the first steps of young Octavian on his way to the top, with the crucial support of none other than Cicero. These were indeed decisive years in the history of Rome. This book will deal with the Republic's struggle for survival and with Cicero's role in it.

Cicero's distinction as a man of letters tends to obscure the fact that all his life he wanted nothing more than to be a statesman. It may seem tragic that in this role he failed more often than he succeeded (although in politics, too, he definitely had his moments) and that he achieved immortality by doing what he regarded as only a substitute for politics. His contributions to the theory and practice of rhetoric, ethics, the theory of perception, theology, law, language, style, and literary dialogue are both numerous and fundamental. It was Cicero who made Greek philosophy accessible to a wider Roman public, and, more important, to the medieval world, by creating the Latin terms capable of expressing the meaning of the Greek ones and by widely discussing Greek philosophy in Latin. Still, fully conscious and proud as he was of his achievements in these areas, he himself considered them only small consolation for his inability to do what he really wanted to do: play an important role in politics and earn glory as a political leader of the Republic. Almost all of his philosophical, rhetorical, and theoretical writings were produced while he was forced to abstain from any active role in politics, that is to say, from 54 to 51 (during the predominance of Pompey and Caesar) and again from 46 to 44 B.C. (while Caesar was dictator). Cicero explicitly states more than once that politics were his absolute priority, leisure and scholarship only a stopgap.

To be sure, some remarks of his seem to contradict this statement, insofar as he occasionally praises the *bios theoretikos* (or the *vita contemplativa*) as the most desirable form of life. Such remarks date mainly from the years of Caesar's dictatorship and should not deceive anyone. They cannot be taken as Cicero's true conviction, since more than once, as soon as he saw an opportunity to return to the political arena, he abandoned such a stance. He expressed his real convictions in the fall of 44 B.C., some months after Caesar's murder, when he felt free to do so and was not far from entering the political scene once more. The passage in *De divinatione* (II 6–7) reads as follows: "The cause of my becoming an expounder of philosophy sprang from the grave condition of the State during the period of Civil War, when being unable to protect the Republic, as had been my custom, and finding it impossible to remain inactive, I could find nothing else that I preferred to do that was worthy of me. . . . When the last named fate [Caesar's monarchy] had befallen my country, and I had been debarred from my former activities, I began to cultivate anew these present studies that by their means, rather than by any other, I might relieve my mind of its worries and at the same time serve my fellow-countrymen as best I could under the circumstances."

This is but one of several clear indications that for Cicero politics were his priority, scholarly work only a second best.[2] More than once, when he despaired of reasonable political activity, he turned to his study and to his books; whenever he regained hope for a role in politics, he turned his back on books.[3] Since he preferred politics, Cicero himself invites the historian to assess his performance in Roman politics.

This assessment, done often from antiquity[4] to modern times, has not always been done dispassionately, since the personality that comes across through Cicero's writings, speeches, and particularly letters arouses strong emotions. From the beginning of modern scholarship in the first half of the nineteenth century, the result of such assessment was nothing short of devastating for Cicero, and remained so for some time. It more or less started with an enormously detailed study of the late Republic by Wilhelm Drumann. The work is arranged as a history of the great and influential Roman clans, and Cicero, together with the other members of the gens Tullia, is dealt with in volumes 5 and 6, published in Königsberg in 1841 and 1844, respectively.[5] There are some 1,200 pages on Cicero alone! Drumann's extremely hostile verdict was soon repeated, in the most forceful language, by the young Theodor Mommsen. Mommsen's idol was Julius Caesar, whom he considered the perfect statesman and a model human being.[6] By contrast, one of Caesar's most serious opponents, Cicero, became the villain par excellence, the opposite of all the attributes that made Caesar great. The question of how to evaluate Cicero in comparison with Caesar will be discussed in the final chapter, but it may be noted here that Paul Groebe, who in 1897 began to revise Drumann's work, wanted to make substantial changes. He failed because of "the invincible and extremely pungent opposition of Mommsen, who having based his account on Drumann's did not even want to see a single word of the text changed, much less the nature of the whole work."[7]

On the other hand, both Cicero the man and Cicero the politician have found advocates. Gaston Boissier did much to vindicate him in a famous book, *Cicéron et ses amis,* first published in 1865. Another effective advocate was the Latin scholar Richard Heinze, whose paper on Cicero's political beginnings, published in 1909, refuted Mommsen's charge that Cicero was nothing but an opportunist who gained office after office posing as a reformer, only to reveal his true colors, those of a reactionary, once he had secured the highest rank, the consulate. Although Heinze destroyed the myth of Cicero the political weathervane, the myth, as it happens, still persists. Many other scholars have contributed to a different, much more positive picture of Cicero the politician: among them Emanuele Ciaceri in the 1920s; more recently, Matthias Gelzer,

Richard Edwin Smith, David Stockton, Kazimierz Kumaniecki, Hermann Strasburger, Elizabeth Rawson, Maria Bellincioni, and Klaus Girardet.[8] The tradition of Drumann and Mommsen, however, is still alive in other quarters, the principal authority being the late Andreas Alföldi, whose admiration for Caesar rivalled that of Mommsen and who sees in Cicero the despicable enemy of a great and creative genius.[9] Others could easily be named, for instance Lloyd Thompson with his paper of 1962, "Cicero the Politician." Among those more than moderately opposed to Cicero, one might also count Sir Ronald Syme, dispassionate as his criticism may sound—this is as deceptive as Tacitus's seemingly dispassionate comments are.[10] Not long ago, one of the foremost experts on the late Roman republic, Christian Meier, who cannot readily be accused of hostility toward Cicero, still rendered the following severe judgment on him: "it was mainly his vanity and also a special, unpolitical manner of thinking that made him aim for many things that were impossible to achieve. Furthermore, his substance was in no way equal to his position, the less so, since he knew little of political tactics, not much more of political judgment. To put it bluntly, he was no politician."[11]

While Meier's essay is well worth reading, these statements seem quite wrong. In this instance, the author by far overshoots his target. First of all, Cicero's way of thinking was, on the contrary, primarily and thoroughly political, although different from that of Caesar or that of Cato. While Caesar possessed an unfailing instinct for power, Cato was guided by strong principles and always opposed to compromise. Cicero's mind was no less politically oriented than theirs, but worked in a different way: less blunt and less direct, always reflecting, often unsure of its direction. Second, the charge that Cicero knew little about political tactics seems absurd, in light of his unparalleled rise from obscurity to prominence or the methods by which, in 43 B.C., he forced his political strategy upon an indifferent or reluctant Senate and for some eight months was the unofficial, but real leader of the Republic. As for his ability to judge politics, he did err often, but more often still he clearly analyzed the political situation of the day and accurately foretold future developments. Countless letters testify to this ability. Furthermore, to say that his substance as a politician was not equal to his position as a *vir consularis,* a former consul, is odd indeed. This can only be maintained if Cicero is measured by a different yardstick than his peers, most of whom he outshone in the way he conducted himself most of the time (admittedly, not always). Finally, the verdict that he was no politician is hard to accept. The aim of this book is to show that this view is incorrect. How else can one explain that, on the eve of the Civil War, in the fall of 50 B.C., no other Roman citizen was courted as much as Cicero by both protagonists, Caesar and Pompey: both recognized him to be a special political force. Cicero, to be sure, was first and foremost a politician.[12]

There is, of course, a kernel of truth in Meier's verdict. Cicero was very different from the conventional Roman politician type. He was not of noble birth and had no senatorial ancestors; he was born in a country town (Arpinum) and into an equestrian family; he was an intellectual with few important connections and no influential clients at the beginning of his career. It was never his style to further his political goals by spending money: to begin with, he had no large fortune, and he did not plunder provinces as many other senators did—Caesar prominent among them. He did not try to attract followers by busily writing new laws. He abhorred military service and war. As he himself once put it, in his unique manner: "No man is less timid than I, yet no man is more cautious."[13] All of that is to say that he was heavily handicapped for a political career; he lacked some of the qualities and attributes Roman noblemen had and valued. He could not avail himself of distinguished ancestors who had been consuls or censors and had celebrated triumphs. However, he could have distinguished himself, as Marius had done, in the army. He could have made a fortune, within a year or two, by exploiting a province, but twice, when it was his turn to become a provincial governor, he chose not to. Given these idiosyncracies of his, it was unavoidable that once in a while he stumbled and made mistakes that some noticed and held against him; for instance, when already a member of the Roman Senate, he not only addressed the town council of Syracuse in Sicily (a subject city), but moreover did so in Greek, as only an intellectual parvenu would do; the aristocratic clan of the Metelli called such a slip nothing short of a crime: *indignum facinus.*[14]

Cicero never learned several things regarded as proper for a Roman senator: he was always active and always talkative, even when wisdom or circumstances called for inactivity and silence. He could never suppress the biting joke that occurred to his quick mind, a habit that sometimes earned him enmity amidst the cheers. He often pushed himself into the foreground, when restraint and a backstage position would have served him better and been more decent.[15] Obviously, these shortcomings resulted from the difference between his background and that of the aristocrats, who looked back on a long row of senatorial ancestors and consuls and who could remain passive or lie low in critical situations without damaging their image; men for whom new honors and new assignments were waiting at the right time, while Cicero always had to make a special effort to attain them. Despite his weaknesses and despite the differences in his outlook from that of the conventional Roman *nobilis,* Cicero nearly always proved equal to the high positions which he had reached.

Also, with regard to Christian Meier's verdict that Cicero was no politician, it must be admitted that serious personal deficiencies prevented him from becoming a great politician (a "statesman"). But it could be argued that he might nevertheless have been a leader in Roman politics for many years (such as, for instance, Marcus Aemilius Scaurus had been at the time of Cicero's birth). His greatest misfortune was that he had to face two uniquely gifted opponents. In the course of only fifteen years of his political career (from 59 to 44 B.C.), he faced first Caesar, and then Octavian, two of the three geniuses of power which the Roman Republic produced (the third being Sulla, whom young Cicero in 81 B.C. just marginally confronted). During these fifteen years, only a few months in 44 B.C. following Caesar's murder had no strong impact from one or the other of the two. And it was precisely during those months that Cicero became the leader of the state. It is true that both defeated him, but this hardly proves that he was no politician. It proves that as a politician he was not their equal—but after all, who was? And since these two were responsible for the most important decisions of the time, it is quite correct to say of Cicero: "the most substantial decisions happened without and against him."[16]

Even so, the words "against him" are indicative; indicative that it was Cicero who represented the opposition no less than Pompey or Cato in Caesar's case, and no less than Brutus and Cassius in Octavian's. Only prejudice can deny that Cicero, despite all his weaknesses and lack of robustness, deserves a prominent place among the political leaders of the time.

While Cicero the politician is still (and will always remain) a topic worth discussing, to extenuate his shortcomings in this role would serve no purpose. They are indisputable, and the severest witness for the prosecution is most often Cicero himself. However, they can and should be balanced by his virtues, which many scholars often fail to notice or to appreciate adequately. For a scholar who enjoys a sheltered position at his desk, where no question of life and death is at stake, it is easy enough to poke fun at a politician who vacillates in critical situations. It is easy, but it is not fair.

Before looking more closely into Cicero's political career, it may be worthwhile to sketch the background by recapitulating some essential features of the period in which Cicero grew up and looking at the general conditions of Roman politics in the years after Sulla's restoration of 82 B.C., when, in 76, at the age of thirty, Cicero made his first bid for public office.[17]

Cicero was born early in 106 B.C., some ten months before Pompey and six years before Caesar. His birth came at the eve of Marius's triumph over King Jugurtha of Numidia and the disastrous defeat of two consular armies in Gaul. Both events happened in 105 B.C., only two of many that made the period one of such change and turmoil that several scholars speak of an age of revolution.[18] Some even do so for the time before Cicero was born (as did Mommsen, defining the years from 133 to Sulla's restoration in 81 B.C. as the age of revolution); others do so only for the period of Cicero's maturity (as did Asinius Pollio, his younger contemporary, and in our time Sir Ronald Syme); for them the Roman revolution began in 60 B.C. with the secret pact of three, the so-called first triumvirate. Other scholars vigorously deny that what evolved over thirty, fifty, or even one hundred years can be called a revolution. Most, however, would concede that from the time of the Gracchi to the battle of Actium, from 133 to 31 B.C., the Roman Republic was almost continually in a state of crisis. Christian Meier has impressed many with his thesis that it was a crisis without an alternative ("Krise ohne Alternative")[19] and therefore had to end in civil war and monarchy. Others do not see a severe crisis at all and vehemently dispute that the Civil War and the collapse of the Republic were long predetermined; for them the outcome resulted from a number of unfortunate coincidences that prematurely caused the death of the Republic. The principal spokesman for this view is Erich Gruen, whose thesis is that, up to the eve of civil war in the fall of 50 B.C., tradition prevailed to the extent that it was mainly "business as usual."[20] There is no need here to enter the debate about whether, or from when, the Republic was doomed to collapse. Nevertheless, it is undeniable that from Tiberius Gracchus's tribunate in 133 B.C. to Sulla's restoration of senatorial power in 81, Roman politics went through one crisis after another; that for a decade Sulla brought relative stability which then gave way, once the political leverage of the tribunate was reactivated in 70 B.C., to another wave of increasingly serious crises, until Julius Caesar, for his personal aims, went to war against the Republic in January 49.

The common denominator in the main developments during the generation before Cicero was born was that new elements entered the political scene and, for the first time, disputed the Senate's claim to exclusive rule. Groups of citizens that had up to then been indifferent or at least not articulate toward politics, and individual members of the nobility, emerged as new political forces to be reckoned with. Others were the new army, reformed by Marius, and the Roman allies in Italy who lacked Roman citizenship and were treated as subjects rather than as allies. More specifically, both Tiberius and his younger brother Gaius Sempronius Gracchus, during their tribunates (133 and 123–122, respectively), had given the urban masses the feeling that, through their numbers and their votes in the assembly, they could express and attain political goals, provided a man qualified to put bills before the assembly (such as the higher magistrates and the tribunes) dared to do so against the Senate's wishes. Gaius Gracchus then made the poorer strata of the capital eligible to buy grain at a reduced price, using social policy to create an army of political followers. He also carried through a reform of the law courts that made the knights the judges of senators in those criminal cases in which a senator was accused of having abused his official trust, and especially a governor at the expense of the provincial population *(quaestio de repetundis)*. With this, he stirred up enmity between the aristocracy and the knights. Up to then the latter had been an unpolitical group of landowners and businessmen. Now, they not only were politicized, but also emerged as a distinct class: Gaius Gracchus even gave them class insignia to underscore this fact. He was fully aware of what he was doing, since he is reported to have said that with the reform of the jury, he had thrown the dagger onto the forum with which the two upper classes would lacerate each other.[21]

The political landscape changed considerably as a consequence of these and other reforms. Whereas for centuries an elite of aristocrats had governed without opposition, other groups now appeared ready to stand up for their own aims and their particular interests, aided by some aristocrats who wished to use them for personal political goals. Although the nobility managed, through violent actions of doubtful legality, to crush the two Sempronian brothers and their followers, the first in 132, the second in 121 B.C., and to redress some of their legislation, they could not completely smother the new political elements. And whenever the aristocracy blatantly failed in its duties, these new groups were prepared to join forces and overpower the ruling class. This they did when, after a series of senatorial corruption scandals and defeats in battle, knights and plebs concluded an alliance and pushed their candidate Gaius Marius to the consulate for 107 B.C. and into the command against King Jugurtha. Like Cicero later, Marius was an upstart, a "new man" *(homo novus)*, born, by coincidence, at Arpinum. After his victory, his followers had Marius elected every year from 104 to 100, to five more consulships, until he also defeated the German tribes against which earlier commanders of the nobility had disgracefully failed.

These victories were due only to the effects of a military reform that Marius had pushed through. Whereas the Gracchi, through their agrarian bills, had attempted to strengthen the ailing farmer class, traditionally the backbone of the Roman army, and thereby to restore the strength and efficiency of the army as an army of landowners, Marius, on the contrary, built the new army by appealing to those who owned nothing, the *proletarii*. He attracted men who came to the service to earn a living and, possibly, booty. This had important consequences: the new soldiers volunteered, they were not drafted. They were no longer amateurs who after a campaign hastened home to their farms, but professionals who had to be fed throughout the year, in peace as well as in war, and who thus became very dependent on their commander's ability to provide them with their daily needs, and with a living once they were no longer fit to serve. This was usually a piece of land which the Senate had to allocate. All this created a new bond between army and general and a tendency for the soldiers to value their loyalty to their commander above their loyalty to the state, or to turn against their commander if he was unable to satisfy their needs. In short, the army, too, became politically conscious, even more so than the knights and the proletariat of the capital, and politically active. With the new Marian army, another pressure group was created which, in case of conflict, tended to put its own interests first.[22]

Finally, there were the Italian allies of the Romans, the *socii*. In the later second century B.C., they contributed about two-thirds of the total strength of the Roman army, but, lacking Roman citizenship, they were grossly underprivileged in their legal status, whether as soldiers or as civilians, and were often exposed to harassment from Roman magistrates and even from Roman matrons. The lack of equal rights for people doing equal duties with the Romans created animosity. Several attempts to enfranchise the Italians were made (beginning again with the Gracchan brothers), but failed because of the violent opposition of the urban masses. They were afraid of losing, and unwilling to share, their privileges,

11

such as the grain subventions. In the end, the Italians went to war (90–88 B.C.) and earned their citizenship, the Romans acceding to the demand in order to survive and regain control. From this time on, Italy, from the Straits of Messina in the south, to the Po and the Rubicon in the north, was the territory of Roman citizens, whereas those living north of the river, the Transpadani or Cisalpini ("those beyond the Po" or "on this side of the Alps") retained their former, lesser status as provincials, that is to say, as subjects.

Civil War immediately followed the settlement with the Italians. It began in 88 B.C. and was caused by problems connected with the massive franchise granted to the Italians as well as by events in Asia Minor. The protagonists were the consul Lucius Cornelius Sulla and the tribune Publius Sulpicius Rufus. Sulpicius made himself the advocate of the new citizens in an issue of vital importance: whether all or only a few of the thirty-five voting units (*tribus*) would be open to receive them. If only a few, their very large numbers would affect only a few of the thirty-five votes. In his efforts to attain a generous solution Sulpicius was joined by Gaius Marius. Their main opponent was Sulla, once a subordinate commander of Marius in the war against Jugurtha, but, following the end of that war, his personal foe for many years.

At the same time Rome was facing a very serious challenge in Asia Minor. The king of Pontus, Mithridates VI Eupator, had invaded the Roman province of Asia in 88 B.C., destroyed all Roman forces, and ordered the massacre of all Romans and Italians in Asia Minor. The Senate had entrusted the consul Sulla with the command against him. This was now overturned by Sulpicius who introduced a bill assigning this command to Marius. Sulla, however, ignored the people's will; he turned around the army with which he was wrapping up the Social War against the Italian allies, marched on Rome, and occupied the city. This was the first major manifestation of the fact that Marius's reform had drawn the army into the political arena; the inherent irony was that Marius's foe used the new instrument against its creator.[23] Sulla had the laws of Sulpicius rescinded and the leaders of the opposition declared enemies. Sulpicius was betrayed and executed while Marius managed to escape.

The following year, 87 B.C., witnessed a complete reversal. Sulla had left for Greece to fight Mithridates. Marius returned and joined forces with the consul Cornelius Cinna. The two gained the upper hand, occupied Rome, and ruled, as Sulla had done, through terror. Marius died before long, but Cinna managed to stay in power for several years, until he was killed by men in his own army when he tried to lead them to Greece against Sulla. Sulla, in turn, having defeated Mithridates in a series of battles in Greece (Athens was badly damaged in 86 B.C.) and in Asia Minor, returned in 83 with his victorious army. In a bloody civil war that ravaged Italy in 83 and 82, he defeated his opposition led by the younger Marius. Appointed dictator for the purpose of drafting a new constitution, he first outlawed more than a thousand of his surviving opponents, many knights among them. The properties of the victims were confiscated and auctioned off (these measures are the notorious proscriptions). Sulla then enacted numerous new laws that considerably changed the constitution. By a variety of acts he restored full political control to the Senate: he banned the use of regular armed forces in Italy, he replaced the knights as jurors by senators, and he emasculated the tribunate. He resigned in 80 B.C. and died in 78.

For the young Roman who, like Cicero, came of age during the eighties and wished to pursue a political career, the rules under which competition for offices took place had been drastically altered by Sulla. If such a man had the misfortune of being the son of one of the dictator's outlawed foes, he simply was prohibited from running for office at all. On the other hand, those elected to the lowest office, the quaestorship, were at once, by that very fact, assured of a seat in the Senate which they could occupy as soon as their term of office ended. Once Sulla had devitalized it, the more ambitious candidates would no longer compete for the tribunate of the plebs, until recently so full of political potential: the tribunes could no longer bring bills straight to the people's assembly, but only after they had been approved by the Senate. And whoever served as tribune of the plebs could go no further—he was thereby disqualified for all higher positions.

Moreover, since Sulla had increased the number of praetors

from six to eight, junior politicians had now a slightly better chance to rise to the second highest rank of the senatorial career. And those who made it that far could now confidently count on two consecutive years in office, because there were now about twice as many positions requiring men of the two highest ranks as there were men so qualified—ten every year (two consuls and eight praetors). But by now there were eight or nine provinces that had to be governed by higher magistrates, and in addition to the functions of the two consuls, eight positions in the city had to be filled by praetors, for the various branches of jurisdiction. It therefore became the norm for a higher magistrate to serve for a year in the city, and to go on to govern a province for another year or even several years, if his tenure was extended.

Furthermore, Sulla also increased the number of quaestors from sixteen to twenty annually. As a consequence, more men attained office than ever before (and, through their first office, a seat in the Senate). Competition thus became keener, with the result that those running for office spent greater and greater sums of money on their election campaigns and on the electorate, using legal as well as illegal tactics. An increasing number of candidates became heavily in debt and many, especially those who did not get elected, went bankrupt; those who made it to the praetorship were better off; their credit was extended because they and their creditors knew that within a year they would govern a province. This, in turn, was an opportunity to earn enough money to pay back their debts and still come out with a profit. It is well known that after his praetorship, Caesar's creditors tried to prevent him from leaving for his province in Spain until the superrich Crassus gave them the guarantees they wanted; Caesar returned after a year, not only free of debt but rich enough to compete for the consulship. To be sure, laws intended to prevent illegal practices of gathering votes (laws *de ambitu,* on canvassing for office) existed, but their effect was limited.

For those who wanted to pursue a political career but who were not well connected, only two major avenues existed to enable them to move up to the higher offices: service in the army or spending large amounts of money. Military service could lead to glory and prestige and could also create a nucleus of loyal followers whose votes would come in handy at an election. In the winter of 56/55 B.C., large numbers of Caesar's soldiers in Gaul were given leave for Rome to help secure the election of Pompey and Crassus to the consulship. A military *clientela* could moreover lend armed support to its leader, as the army had done for Sulla in 88, as Caesar's soldiers would do at the Rubicon in January 49, and those of Octavian in the summer of 43, extorting the consulship for their commander.

Money spent on public buildings, on entertainment for the city's population, on grain (to bring down the market price), or on bribes (involving, however, the risk of standing trial and being convicted) could also help a candidate's career. But for those who had not inherited a large fortune, almost the only way of getting rich was exploiting a province as governor. However, such an opportunity presented itself only to those who had already reached the rank of praetor. And not all gave in to such temptation. One might think that a famous attorney, such as Cicero would become, might pile up a fortune from the honoraria of those whom he defended in court, but Roman law prohibited the acceptance of such fees.

It was after Sulla's reforms and under the conditions just briefly described that Marcus Tullius Cicero ventured a public appearance. Sulla had repressed the new elements that had disputed the Senate's dominant role in politics and had reinstated those who traditionally had monopolized power, privileges, and much of the state's wealth. It could easily be foreseen that those deprived or repressed by Sulla would try to regain their position and to reclaim their share. When young Cicero set out to make a career in politics, he had to take a stand amid impending conflicts.

Chapter Two

From Upstart to "Father of His Country"

Marcus Tullius Cicero had his roots in Arpinum, a modest country town located on a steep hill above the Liris valley, about seventy miles southeast of Rome. Later in life, he set his dialogue "On the Laws" at that site, and his description clearly reflects his deep emotional attachment to it. At the time of Cicero's birth in 106 B.C., the inhabitants of Arpinum had enjoyed full Roman citizenship for some eighty years. Local politics was apparently controlled by three ambitious equestrian families, the Marii, the Gratidii, and the Tullii Cicerones, all related by marriage and all competing for influence and power. Apparently, the Marii and the Gratidii were usually well disposed toward new, sometimes radical developments in politics, whereas the Tullii stood for what was sanctioned by tradition. They were the conservatives.[1]

When young Cicero became a teenager, around 95 B.C., the family left Arpinum to settle in Rome, where his father had bought a house for the chief purpose of allowing his sons, Marcus and the younger Quintus, to receive the best possible education and move ahead in the world. The family's few connections with members of the aristocracy could now be exploited. Cicero's grandfather had been commended in 115 B.C. by the leader of the Senate, Marcus Aemilius Scaurus, for the stand he took against his brother-in-law Gratidius in a matter of local politics (but with wider implications) that had eventually come to the Senate's attention. This must have opened some doors to his offspring. In any event, the two boys were introduced to some very cultivated noblemen, especially the two outstanding orators, Lucius Licinius Crassus and Marcus Antonius, to Quintus Mucius Scaevola the augur, and to his cousin's homonymous son, Scaevola the pontifex. The latter two men were the leading authorities in civil and sacred law. Scaevola the pontifex was consul in 95 B.C. together with Crassus, and governor of Asia, apparently the following year, in what was to remain forever the model of a fair and just rule over a Roman province.[2] To say that young Cicero "studied" rhetoric and law with these men means that he followed them around, was in their suite, and observed day after day what they did and how they did it: when they prepared and delivered speeches, how they advised those who sought counsel in matters of law, and how they conducted themselves as prominent figures of the nobility in their contacts with magistrates, other aristocrats, and members of the lower classes.

When in 89 B.C. the Italians went to war against Rome, Cicero, now seventeen, was called up to serve against them, first under the consul Pompeius Strabo (Pompey's father) in Picenum, then under the new consul Sulla in Campania. It was the only military experience he was ever to have, except for his nominal command as governor of Cilicia almost forty years later. As Livy one day would say of him, he was everything else rather than born for war, "vir nihil minus quam ad bella natus."[3] The war hardly over, he was allowed to leave the army and resume his education in Rome. In addition to those whom he constantly followed, he also learned from other famous speakers by attending trials at the forum during which they spoke as attorneys for one party or the other, and by joining political gatherings *(contiones)* at which politicians addressed the crowds on the issues of the day. Extremely popular in 88 B.C. were the *contiones* of the tribune Publius Sulpicius Rufus, the ally of Marius and the Italians, and the foe of Sulla. Sulpicius, who was to perish while still in office, enormously impressed Cicero with his rhetorical ability, but shocked him with his radical politics.

Nothing whatever is known of Cicero during the civil war years. He was "sheltered by insignificance."[4] When Sulla finally restored the conservative nobility to power in 82, many of their best men were dead, including the two famous orators. Lucius Crassus died in 91, on the eve of the war against the Italians, and Scaevola the augur in 87. Marcus Antonius fell victim to the terror in 87, and Scaevola the pontiff suffered the same fate as late as 82 B.C.: he was killed by order of the consul, the younger Marius, just before the latter was himself defeated and executed by Sulla. Scaevola had remained in Rome and had not taken up arms, since he was convinced that civil war was worse than anything.[5] It is impossible to say whether his example guided young Cicero (who venerated him) and made him refrain from any active part in these turbulences. In later life Cicero stated more than once that he shared Scaevola's conviction.

Cicero continued his education as best he could in rhetoric and law, but also (and this was much less common) in philosophy. In 88 B.C., the leader of Plato's Academy, Philo of Larisa, fled Athens, which had sided with Mithridates against the Romans, and stayed in Rome to teach. So did one of the leading Epicureans, Phaedrus. Their teachings and that of the stoic Diodotus strongly influenced Cicero, who acquired during these years much of his broad and precise knowledge of philosophy and the various philosophical systems.

As he himself said, Cicero was determined from his boyhood on to make a career in politics and become a leader. He took as his motto the exhortation to Glaucus and Achilles by their fathers, according to Homer: "Far to excel, out-topping all the rest!"[6] It was not an obvious goal for a young man, however talented, not born in a senatorial family, an outsider of equestrian and small-town birth. Moreover, Cicero was not the man to smooth his difficult path by performing exemplary military service, as Marius had done, the other parvenu from Arpinum. Cicero did not bear a famous name; he had to make a name for himself, and since military glory was not for him, the only other approach that suited him was to become known to the public as an attorney. It was for that reason, he himself reports, that he devoted the days and nights of his youth to the study of eloquence.[7] Highly ambitious and full of drive, he nevertheless took his time and carefully avoided a premature start. He was already twenty-five years old when he appeared in court for the first time, to represent Publius Quinctius, a businessman suing his partner Sextus Naevius. The matter at stake had its roots in the past, the time of the Civil War, and thus had some political implications. Naevius had the support of a very important figure of the nobility, Lucius Marcius Philippus, a former consul and censor; his attorney was Quintus Hortensius, the outstanding orator of the time. Moreover, the praetor, Gnaeus Cornelius Dolabella, a protégé of the dictator Sulla, had already rendered a preliminary ruling favorable to Naevius. With all that against him, the stakes for a young man such as Cicero were quite high. But Cicero was equal to the task and did not shrink from sharply attacking the praetor and his unjust ruling: "Following the practice of members of the nobility, who, when once they have begun to carry out some plan, whether right or wrong, show such superiority in its execution that it is beyond the reach of one in our humble position, Dolabella most manfully persevered in acting wrongfully."[8]

Perhaps the most remarkable feature of this event was that Cicero was already twenty-five years old when he made his debut. His mentor Crassus had only been twenty when he brought to trial a powerful figure, the former consul Gaius Papirius Carbo, in 119 B.C., and secured his condemnation (Carbo took his own life).[9] And Hortensius, Cicero's distinguished opponent in 81, delivered, at age nineteen, a remarkable speech in favor of the province of Africa, before two very competent judges, the consuls of 95, Crassus and Scaevola pontifex. This took place in the Senate and immediately established Hortensius's fame.[10] Cicero must have had good reasons to wait so much longer. True enough, these were the years of the rule of the party of Marius and Cinna, then the years of the Civil War. Conditions were not auspicious for a beginner. However, numerous lawsuits took place during those years, in which others established or strengthened their reputation—Cicero himself mentions Hortensius, Publius Antistius, Marcus Pupius Piso, Gnaeus Pomponius, and others.[11] He could have done the same, had he wanted to—there were enough unpolitical lawsuits to help him build connections and become known to the public. Since he decided to wait so much longer, he must have felt that he was not ready. As he expressed it later: "It was not until this time that I first began to undertake cases both civil and criminal, for it was my ambition, not (as most do) to learn my trade in the forum, but so far as possible to enter the forum already trained."[12]

His performance in the civil case of Quinctius was the beginning of a rapid forensic career. Soon after, influential aristocrats chose him for his first criminal lawsuit: he was to defend Sextus Roscius of Ameria, accused of having murdered his own father. The case was closely connected with the terror of the proscriptions. The victim had been murdered in 81 B.C., several months after the official termination of the proscriptions. Two of his estranged relatives informed Sulla's favorite, the freedman L. Cornelius Chrysogonus, about this. Chrysogonus, described by Cicero as possibly the most powerful man of the time, managed to illegally insert the name of the murdered Roscius (who had been a partisan of Sulla) into the list of those outlawed by Sulla earlier. That enabled him to confiscate the victim's large fortune, acquire it for almost nothing, and reward his informants. Through a delegation to Sulla, the town council of Ameria tried to have an inquiry performed, but Chrysogonus was able to thwart these efforts. The victim's son, meanwhile, had fled to Rome. The conspirators, worried that he might raise difficulties for them, took the initiative and accused him of having murdered his father, fully expecting that no one would dare to stand up for him against the powerful Chrysogonus and that the trial would be a farce or, as Cicero puts it, a holdup.[13]

The scheme backfired. Young Roscius had influential friends among several aristocratic families, willing to help but themselves too exposed to take on the risky business. They selected Cicero, who was young and unimportant enough to get away with saying what had to be said. The trial (in 80 B.C.) took place before a jury of senators (Sulla had just removed the knights and reinstated senatorial jurors). Proving the absurdity of the murder charge against young Roscius was relatively easy. However, exposing the role of Chrysogonus and discussing the awesome proscriptions was a delicate task. Cicero was very careful to separate Sulla from Chrysogonus, to praise the dictator while condemning his henchman. Sulla, he explained, had no part and no knowledge of such crimes committed in his name. He had restored law and justice in Rome, and it was now up to the jury to prove that this was no empty claim, that the dark times of Civil War, proscriptions, and lawlessness (88–82 B.C.) were at an end and that, with the senators back as jurors, justice had returned to the courtrooms.

The defendant was acquitted, the trial a big success for Cicero, further consolidated and enhanced by the publication of the speech.[14] Although it has been questioned whether Sulla was, in fact, still dictator at the time of the trial, that seems almost certain.[15] In any event, Cicero displayed great courage in dealing with the events of recent years in the way he did. With victory in this case, he made a name for himself. Business started to boom, influential people required his services and repaid Cicero with their support and that of their clients whenever he needed it. After some time, he felt tired and went abroad for two years (79–77 B.C.) to Greece, Rhodes, and Asia Minor, mainly for health reasons (he needed to improve his speaking technique), but also to continue learning from Greek orators and philosophers.[16] With him went his brother Quintus, his friend Titus Pomponius—later called Atticus because of his love and benefactions for Athens—and other friends. In Athens they attended the classes of Antiochus of Ascalon, the head of the Academy, and those of two prominent Epicureans, Zeno and Phaedrus.[17] Pomponius Atticus, a few years Cicero's senior, who came himself from a family of wealthy knights, became an Epicurean, while Cicero remained basically a follower of Plato's Academy. Epicurus's doctrine that the wise man should take no part in politics suited Atticus but was not for Cicero; to keep a low profile was not his intention; he was determined to be a leader.

After his return in 77 B.C., important cases kept him busy once again. But while it seemed appropriate to sketch Cicero's first steps in public life, it may be enough now, for the next stages of his career, to mention only a few highlights instead of following closely every step, since only with the consulate did a man acquire weighty political leverage.[18] The consulate was Cicero's goal and he was methodical in its pursuit. He was careful not to arouse enmities, and for many years he appeared in court only to defend people, not once to indict and prosecute. He was also very cautious not to offend the influential circles of the nobility, a member of which he was determined to become, against all odds. At the age of thirty, he was elected quaestor and served, in 75 B.C., in western Sicily. On a visit to the eastern part of the province, he searched in Syracuse for the tomb of Archimedes, who had been slain by a Roman soldier in 211 B.C., when the city was taken by storm during the Hannibalic War. Although the spot was neglected and hard to find, Cicero discovered it.[19]

When his year of office ended, he became, according to a rule instituted by Sulla, a member of the Senate, among the *viri quaestorii*—that is to say, the lowest of the four ranks of senators. He is attested as such in an inscription from Oropus, at the border between Attica and Boeotia, in a decree of the Senate of 73 B.C. This concerned the sanctuary of the hero Amphiaraus and the Roman tax farmers *(publicani)*, who wanted to tax the sacred land and argued that it was, in fact, not sacred, because Amphiaraus was not a god, but only a hero. The consuls discussed the matter with a consilium of senatorial advisers, one of whom was Cicero, and then reported on it to the full Senate. The Senate decided against the tax farmers.[20] Cicero did not compete to become tribune of the plebs, because Sulla had made the tribunate the dead end of a political career. He was, however, elected aedile for the year 69 B.C. and praetor for 66; as praetor, it fell to him to preside over the court which heard cases of exploitation by provincial governors *(quaestio de repetundis)*. He had by now made his way up to the second rank of senators. Details will follow, but his career proceeded thus: consul in 63 and a life member of the collegium of augurs in 53. He was unsuccessful in his bid for the censorship, although he once had hoped to reach that position; he did not run in 55 and was unable to run the next time, in 50, since he was then governor of the province of Cilicia in southeastern Asia Minor.[21]

Such a career, or *cursus honorum,* was quite normal for a Roman nobleman. It was, however, nothing short of sensational for a newcomer of equestrian and provincial birth. While it was not too difficult for such a man to get elected to a quaestorship and thereby to become a Roman senator, only very few succeeded in securing higher offices. For those who did, the position of praetor, at the very best, was the end of the road. The last *homo novus* who had managed to reach beyond that barrier to the consulate had been Gaius Coelius Caldus in 94 B.C.[22] After him, sixty more consuls had been elected before another newcomer, Cicero, achieved victory. And Cicero owed his success almost exclusively to his own merit, although in the later stages of his bid for the consulship he received the support of members of the aristocracy who were afraid of his competitor Catilina.[23]

The singular pattern of his career with respect to his origins was always present in Cicero's mind. Legitimate pride and the subliminal feeling of suffering from a defect combined to create a peculiar tension. Significant in this respect is a passage from a letter written much later, in 50 B.C., to Appius Claudius Pulcher, a distinguished member of the high aristocracy, which reads as follows: "Do you suppose that any Appiety or Lentulity counts more with me than the ornaments of merit? Even before I gained the distinctions which the world holds highest, I was never dazzled by aristocratic names; it was the men who bequeathed them to you that I admired. But after I won and filled positions of the highest authority in such a fashion as to let me feel no need of additional rank or fame, I hoped to have become the equal (never the superior) of you and your peers."[24] This is the language of a parvenu; nevertheless, Cicero had good reasons to be proud. He interpreted his success as the triumph of personal virtues, while others acquired the consulate simply by being nobly born. The rule, he once said, was that some were made consuls in the cradle.[25] He meant those born as an Aemilius, Aurelius, Caecilius, Calpurnius, Claudius, Cornelius, or as a Domitius, Licinius, Lutatius, a Manlius, Marcius,

Servilius, or Valerius. It was as much of a sensation for a Tullius from Arpinum to become consul, as it was in 55 B.C. for a Domitius Ahenobarbus to fail when it was to be his year: "Could anything be more lamentable than for a man who has been consul-designate from his cradle to be debarred from becoming consul?"[26] Domitius's failure, to be sure, was the result of extraordinary circumstances: the combined forces of the triumviri intervened; Pompey and Crassus had the elections postponed through various maneuvers, until, after a delay of six months, their partner Julius Caesar could give his soldiers leave to go to Rome and secure their election. In fact, the unfortunate Domitius had to wait until the following year to reach the highest office.

Still another dimension of Cicero's triumph is the fact that he was elected to all his offices at his first attempt, and that he secured them all in the very first year he became eligible for them (*legitimo anno* or *suo anno*). That was a unique success.[27] Not even the great Marius, his fellow-countryman from Arpinum, had been able to do that: he failed twice in his bid to become aedile, and when he ran for the praetorship, he barely made it, as the last of the candidates elected—and immediately ran into trouble. Marius was accused of having bribed the electorate and had a narrow escape (just as many jurors found him guilty as found him innocent—and his jurors were his equestrian peers!). No such stain blemished any stage of Cicero's career; on the contrary, he was among the first to be elected quaestor, the first as aedile, the first again as praetor, and the first as consul: he received the votes of all the voting units (the *centuriae*), while their votes for the second consul were split.

A few figures will illustrate how keen competition for offices really was and how it increased from the lower to the higher positions. Twenty quaestors were elected every year, all of whom entered the Senate after their term of office expired. Only fourteen of them could secure the next level, that of either tribune or aedile, and only eight the following level, the office of praetor, a prerequisite and the stepping-stone for the consulate. Not more than two of the eight (or of the original twenty) would reach the highest office. No wonder, therefore, that the families which counted consuls among their members made every effort to prevent outsiders from rising that far, since every successful newcomer would exclude one of their number. Sergius Catilina (a *patricius*, a man of the highest nobility) was not alone in resenting the fact that Cicero was elected to a place he thought rightfully his. All candidates, once they failed, had only a very slim chance of making it in a later year. They were burdened with a rejection (*repulsa*), and every year a new crop of eight ex-praetors waited for their chance. Moreover, the censors of 70 B.C. expelled no less than sixty-four members from the Senate, most of whom again started competing for office in order to regain a seat in the Senate. Thus, competition in the sixties was even keener than usual.

It was indeed a long and difficult road that led Cicero from his first criminal case win in 80 B.C. to his first election to office in 76 and then, step by step, to his election to consul in the summer of 64. He had already traveled a little more than half that distance when he scored a major triumph which greatly helped his career: the trial of Gaius Verres in 70 B.C. The case made the already well-known attorney a celebrity and, since Hortensius, the "king of the forum," was the defendant's advocate, Cicero's victory established him in Hortensius's place as the foremost orator in Rome. Gaius Verres had been governor of Sicily for three consecutive years, from 73 to 71, and had far exceeded other bad governors. He was as cruel as he was rapacious; he was quoted as saying that his first year's loot was for himself, that of the second year for his attorneys, and that of the third year for his jurors.[28] If true, it meant that he anticipated not only his indictment, but also his acquittal, since he could afford to hire the best advocates and to bribe at least half the jurors.

Without rehashing the details of the affair (they can be found in the several hundred pages of Cicero's speeches against Verres, of which only the first two parts were actually delivered),[29] it should be stated that the case, while presenting risks and enormous difficulties, also held out the possibility of considerable political gains for Cicero. If he failed, his political career was over. When asked by the Sicilians to represent them, he had no choice but to accept, since from the days of his quaestorship in Sicily, the bond of loyalty between the parties made it imperative for Cicero to accede. Therefore, he had to lay aside his principle only to defend people in court; for the first (and the last) time, he acted for the plaintiffs. The fact that Verres's crimes were so many, so serious, and so obvious was to his advantage. Furthermore, because of public dissatisfaction with senatorial juries, a reform to expel the senators from the courts or, at least, to drastically reduce their number was expected at any moment.[30] Moreover, the powerful Roman businessmen lobby was hostile to Verres.

On the other hand, Cicero faced grave obstacles: first of all in the general unwillingness of the senatorial order to see one of their number convicted. Then there was Verres's money, which could be used in an effort to bribe a number of jurors. And Verres had influential friends; Hortensius and Publius Cornelius Scipio (later to become Pompey's father-in-law) volunteered to defend him; the powerful clan of the Metelli was heavily engaged to protect him. Of the three brothers Metellus, one took over Sicily from Verres as governor in 70 and made it difficult for Cicero to collect damaging evidence; another brother was running for the consulship, the third for the praetorship in 69, and none other than Verres financed their campaigns. Both were elected a few days before the trial began. Hortensius was also elected to the consulship. In short, Cicero ran into all kinds of trouble, both in Rome and in Sicily. It even looked as if the opposition might succeed in having the proceedings postponed into the following year 69, when the praetor Metellus would be presiding over the court. It was Cicero's circumspection, energy, and wit that thwarted all these efforts. When the hearings began, on 5 August 70 B.C., he made a tactical move that caught Hortensius and the defense completely by surprise. Against all custom, Cicero, after a brief speech, immediately began to call witnesses. The defense was unprepared; public opinion, after the first witnesses were heard, regarded Verres as already convicted and the culprit went into exile before a verdict could be rendered. What Cicero later published under the title of "speeches against Verres" was what he might have said, had the trial run its course; the publication underscored the effect of the case and immortalized it.

The publication of all the collected evidence also made the extent of Verres's crimes more widely known and made those who supported him look bad. Cicero had been careful to depict Verres as atypical. So the nobility, in order not to be identified with him, could do no better than to join public opinion in condemning him. For Cicero, this paid important political dividends: he won immense popularity with the electorate without losing the goodwill of the nobility. He had handled the whole case admirably and given ample proof that his potential as a politician was superior to that of most senators; as *aedile*-elect, he had destroyed the consul-elect Hortensius.

Success did not make him imprudent. He waited another four years before he gave his first public speech outside the courtroom, on a purely political matter. It was in 66 B.C., when he was one of the praetors. His rank was now such that he was expected to have and to express an opinion on major issues. The case in question was the debate on a bill proposed by the tribune Manilius, the *lex Manilia*. The reforms of 70 B.C. had not only deprived the senators of their monopoly to act as jurors, but had removed other elements of Sulla's constitution as well. They had restored the tribunes' prerogative to bring bills directly to the assembly, without the approval, even against the opposition of the Senate. Thereby the conditions were recreated which in 88 B.C. had enabled the tribune Sulpicius Rufus, by that abortive bill of his, to put Marius in Sulla's place as the commander against Mithridates, from which the civil war resulted. The same condition prevailed after 70 B.C. and again allowed for the cooperation of ambitious tribunes with ambitious generals. They allowed the former to secure for the latter, by such popular vote, commands of extraordinary power and duration. This was the method by which Pompey, Caesar, and Crassus, individually and collectively, assumed such power that it made the Republic suffocate. And, since those powerful men had the means to reward those to whom they owed their positions, it was by this method that tribunes such as Gabinius, Vatinius, Clodius, and Trebonius furthered their political career.[31]

In 66 B.C., the tribune Gaius Manilius introduced a bill to give Pompey an extraordinary command against King Mithridates of

Pontus, the war against whom (it was the Third Mithridatic War) had been dragging on for eight years. The year before, another tribune, Aulus Gabinius, had sponsored a similar bill to entrust Pompey with an extraordinary command against the pirates who had become a grave menace. Strong opposition from the leading circles of the nobility, the *optimates* as they called themselves, had led to violence during the voting procedure. Pompey finally received the command and silenced his critics by ending the war in a brief and brilliant campaign. He was now available for the war against Mithridates—he still happened to be in the area and he was, from the viewpoint of military ability, the natural choice. This time, the opposition was much weaker and doomed to failure. Only a few stubborn aristocrats, such as Quintus Catulus and Quintus Hortensius, once more expressed the fear that a man in such a powerful position as the one proposed for Pompey created a threat to the state. Cicero, on the other hand, supported the sponsors of the bill and, in his speech *De lege Manilia* ("On the Bill of Manilius"), recommended its acceptance by the voters. He knew that he would irritate a few of the optimates, but enough were in favor of the bill and, more importantly, so were the voters, among them the influential group of businessmen *(publicani)*; thus, he would also win Pompey's gratitude. This time Cicero could be sure to advance a winning cause.

More and more his thoughts concentrated on winning the consulship, for which he would become eligible in the summer of 64, to take office, if elected, in January 63. He realized that remaining active as an attorney in Rome might win him votes which he could not win were he to govern a province, as was customary in the year following the praetorship. He therefore asked the Senate to be excused and was granted permission. At least for a full year before the actual election, he was preoccupied with the question of who his competitors would be and what were their chances compared to his. His brother Quintus wrote a treatise for him on what to do and what to avoid while running for the highest office, and how to court the electorate. He also advised him not to speak on political issues for the time being, thereby avoiding giving offense to anyone.[32]

When this was written, it became clear that circumstances would be as favorable as they could possibly be. There would be no outstanding candidates this year whose election would be a foregone conclusion. Lucius Sergius Catilina and Gaius Antonius would be the strongest competitors, both influential, but both also, as Quintus reminded his brother, of dubious reputation and viewed with much suspicion in conservative circles. This finally made the outsider Cicero look like the lesser evil in the eyes of many. And Cicero himself capitalized on this, when in a speech as a candidate, he lashed out at their alliance against him, their notorious briberies of the electorate, while depicting himself as a conservative and a safeguard against all undesirable innovations.[33] He came in first, Antonius came in second, only slightly ahead of Catilina.

Once elected to the consulship, Cicero could expect Gaius Antonius to be a difficult colleague, since he had campaigned against Cicero and as an ally of Catilina (both men had been supported by Crassus and Caesar). He could also foresee that Catilina would again run for the consulship, when, shortly after the election, he was acquitted of a murder charge in a trial at which Caesar presided.[34] Under the circumstances, it seemed imperative to secure Antonius's goodwill. Cicero accomplished that cleverly by offering him a chance to acquire wealth and to repay his enormous debts. Immediately after their year of office, the consuls would all govern a province. The Senate was to identify annually which provinces would be those to be governed by the consuls, but had to determine this well in advance, even before the consuls were elected, the idea being to exclude any personal interest. Cicero, therefore, knew before he was elected in the summer of 64 B.C., that in 62 Gallia on this side of the Alps and Macedonia would fall to the next consuls. After the election, the lot gave him Macedonia, a much more lucrative prospect. He offered Antonius an exchange which was gladly accepted. It is alleged in the sources (and possible) that they also tacitly agreed that Cicero would participate in any profits Antonius would make while governor.[35]

The year began with a major struggle that required Cicero's fullest attention. It was caused by an ambitious agrarian bill, sponsored by the tribune Servilius Rullus.[36] Its purpose was to provide farmland to citizens of Rome and to veterans. It was promulgated a few weeks before the beginning of the year 63 (the tribunes took office on 10 December and customarily announced their legislative intentions at once). Cicero, whose offer to help frame the bill had been scornfully rejected, knew well in advance what was coming and was therefore prepared when debate on the bill began in the Senate on 1 January. That very day he delivered the first of four speeches on the new *lex agraria;* others to the people of Rome soon followed. He depicted what seemed a very popular bill as a sinister and dangerous plot to secure royal power by the ten members of a committee scheduled to implement the law. These ten were to be elected for five years and given far-reaching authority. But the elections, Cicero pointed out, would be a farce, since only seventeen of the thirty-five tribes would be called upon to vote, and the votes of only nine tribes would decide the outcome. The bill consequently deprived a majority of the people of their right to vote, and a people's consul such as Cicero could never tolerate such a thing. He also described the ten as no less powerful than kings (a hated word)[37] and criticized the procedures by which they were to be elected. What, for instance, could be the intention of the clause that candidates had to register in person if not to prevent Pompey from being eligible? The popular Pompey, away at war against King Mithridates, was most interested in such a bill for the sake of his veterans.[38]

Reading the second speech on the bill, it is fascinating to see how Cicero managed to arouse the suspicion of the crowd against the sponsors of the bill (in the Senate, he hinted at Crassus and Caesar as the moving spirits behind Rullus). In fact, he convinced the people that, although agrarian legislation was a fine and much needed thing, this law would be pernicious. He got the message across that the sponsors of the bill wrongly pretended to be friends of the people; the people would be better advised to put their trust in him, the people's consul.[39] The bill was withdrawn.

Cicero was, in fact, convinced that this bill was dangerous, but he grossly exaggerated its dangers and intentionally overlooked the great advantages it would have for a large number of citizens.

Be that as it may, his mastery in steering the affair the way he wanted, in the Senate and even more so with the people, is stunning.

The handling of Catilina and his followers was Cicero's greatest triumph—and turned out to be his Waterloo, when several years later it was the cause of his exile. Only the basic facts need be mentioned here. As was expected, in the summer of 63 Catilina ran again for the consulship. Defeated once more, he turned to conspiracy and violence with the intention of overthrowing the government. When it became clear that an army was being recruited for him in Etruria, the Senate called upon the consuls by the so-called "decree of last resort" *(senatus consultum ultimum)* to take all necessary steps for the protection of the state (21 October 63 B.C.). Such an emergency measure had been first used in 121 B.C. against Gaius Gracchus and several times since, and citizens lost their lives in consequence. As the ultimate means of protecting law and order, its legality was not seriously disputed, but public opinion was very watchful of its application: even a consul who had received such a sweeping authorization could be brought to trial and indicted for having done more than what was absolutely necessary; and he might then be either acquitted or condemned.[40] Earlier in 63 had taken place the curious trial of an old senator, Gaius Rabirius, for what he had done in 100 B.C. under similar circumstances. This trial was initiated by Julius Caesar and carried out by the tribune Titus Labienus, Cicero being one of the defendant's lawyers. However bizarre the affair was, thirty-seven years after the incriminating events, under a procedure which, while never rescinded, had long become obsolete, and cut short by some machination without a verdict, it contained a stern warning that the utmost restraint must be used in similar cases of emergency.

When Catilina left Rome in November to join the army of Manlius, the Senate declared these two men public enemies *(hostes)*. A few months later, after Cicero's year as consul had expired, they were defeated and killed in pitched battle. Their fate presented no legal problem. However, others in Rome were a part of the conspiracy, among them senators and even the praetor Publius Lentulus (a former consul).[41] On 3 December, Cicero received proof that their leaders had committed high treason and that they planned an armed revolution. That same day, five men were arrested and led to the Senate, where Cicero presented the evidence against them, documents, and witnesses. The five confessed, their guilt was firmly established, and the Senate formally voted that they had acted against the state.[42] The problem was what to do with them.

This was debated at another meeting held on 5 December. That day, the sixteen most prominent senators, the two *consules designati* and the fourteen *viri consulares* present, all voted in favor of the "ultimate punishment," *ultima poena;* then Julius Caesar, as *praetor designatus,*[43] made a strong case for lifelong custody, whereupon all but one of those who had already voted for capital punishment changed their minds and agreed with him. Only the steadfast Quintus Catulus persevered. Strangely enough, a senator of junior rank, Marcus Cato, then put the senior members of the house to shame by a forceful speech in which he argued that death was the only adequate punishment for the conspirators' crimes. His motion was put to the vote, an overwhelming majority now voting in favor, and Cicero immediately thereafter led the five to their execution. For the moment, almost everyone was in a state of euphoria. Cicero had protected the state in a dangerous situation and had done so with vigilance, circumspection, and courage. The lower strata of the population appreciated this no less than did the members of the senatorial and equestrian orders. Already on 3 December, when the conspirators were arrested and their guilt established, Quintus Catulus, the leader of the optimates, had called Cicero *parens patriae;*[44] another optimate, a former censor, said that Cicero deserved the *corona civica,*[45] a decoration for those who had saved the lives of Roman citizens. The Senate voted a *supplicatio* (a public prayer)—the first ever for a civilian, a *togatus.*[46] After the execution of the conspirators, Cicero received large ovations from the crowd. The scene is vividly depicted in Plutarch's biography of Cicero (chapter 22.5–7); an enthusiastic crowd along the road addressed him as savior and founder of the republic. Led by the high aristocracy, the *homo novus* from Arpinum walked in an unmilitary triumphal procession, universally recognized as the "father of his country."[47]

It is no coincidence that this description is so reminiscent of passages from Cicero himself. Plutarch has embellished the scene (and the whole story of Cicero's consulate) following the latter's own memoir on his consulate, written in 60 B.C. in Greek and distributed throughout Greece by Atticus. This has been convincingly demonstrated by Otto Lendle.[48] One may compare what Cicero says in the third Catilinarian speech: "Since we have raised to the immortal gods that man who founded this city (Romulus-Quirinus), he who preserved this same city ought to be held in honor by you and your posterity."[49] For those who have still not perceived of whom he is talking, he continues: "Now it has been *my* good fortune. . . ." The key words, "savior" and "founder," occur both in this passage and in Plutarch and the effect is, in both instances, to equate Cicero the savior of the city with Romulus, its founder. It had been the custom of the Greeks of old to publicly venerate the founder of a city as a hero, that is to say, a mortal who, by virtue of his deeds, had come close to godlike quality. Greek cities then, especially from Alexander the Great on, voted similar honors for those who had rescued the city from great outside danger or had preserved her from internal revolution. In those cases, the honors were paid to the living and consequently did not qualify as heroic honors. They were identical to those reserved for the gods, and therefore called "godlike honors" (*isotheoi timai*).[50]

Cicero is referring to these concepts whenever he speaks about his consulate and he does so often (as Seneca would put it later: "praised so often not without cause, but without pause"—"illum consulatum suum non sine causa sed sine fine laudatum").[51] Here is just one other passage (from the *De re publica*): "There is, indeed, nothing in which human excellence can more nearly approximate the divine than in the foundation of new states or in the preservation of states already founded."[52]

It is obvious that Cicero regarded his consulate as a divine performance, an *apotheosis*; it had, in fact, been called that by one of the optimates, Scribonius Curio.[53] And in Plutarch's words, "to many of the commanders and generals of the time the Roman people were indebted for wealth and spoils of power, but for preservation and safety to Cicero alone, who had freed them from so peculiar and so great a peril." Plutarch's voice is, in fact, Cicero's own once again, since these sentences are taken from the memoir which Cicero composed on his consulship.[54] The aristocrats, while certainly not going as far as to place Cicero and Romulus on the same level, did fully appreciate what the consul had done; they paid him great honors and even, with the *supplicatio,* unprecedented ones. They were now prepared to accept him as their equal, as one of the political leaders.

For Cicero, however, this was not enough. He was not satisfied to be one among others (even if only a few), and to be consulted on all major affairs of state. He wanted to remain the first or, as he liked to say, remain at the helm. He was unable to see that it was the office that had brought him to the helm for one year and that, after that year ended, he ought to step back into the ranks. So convinced was he that his success was the result of unique personal virtue that he wanted to have this success perpetuated. His superiority, he thought, gave him the right to lead, even without office; not, of course, to give direct orders (which was for the consuls and other magistrates), but by advising those in office, with the expectation that his recommendations would be followed. There was no question in his mind that it was his vocation to steer the course. From the end of his year as consul, this claim is amply attested in his writings and obvious even when he denies making such a claim. The effect such megalomania had on his life was nothing short of ruinous.

Chapter Three

The Princeps Driven into Exile

It has more than once been observed that the consulship was both the climax and the turning point of Cicero's career and that with its expiration the remarkable success story of Cicero's ascending years changed into one of failure.[1] There is much truth in these statements, but, as Shackleton Bailey remarked, Cicero's finest hour was still to come, if only after twenty years of vanity and vexation.[2] On the evening of 5 December 63 B.C., there was nothing but euphoria in the streets of Rome, and Cicero the consul was the man of the hour. The general enthusiasm muted the few dissenting voices. Caesar who had dissented so conspicuously came close to being killed by some enraged knights as he was about to leave the Senate; he had to be protected by his peers. Before long, however, the dissenting voices grew louder and more numerous. They were silenced for the time being by a resolute and still united Senate. But a few years later the dissenters returned in strength and forced Cicero into exile.

The question may be presented as follows: While no one disputed the Senate's authority to punish the five conspirators, not many options were open. During the debate, Julius Caesar alluded to the Sempronian law of Gaius Gracchus which stated that a Roman citizen could not be executed without having been convicted

35

in a people's court.[3] The Senate was neither the people nor a court of law, and a decree of the Senate was not a lawful verdict, but a recommendation of action to be taken by the consul. It was universally acknowledged that those declared public enemies (*hostes*) might be killed with impunity. But only those who had actually taken up arms with Catilina had been so labeled, not the conspirators in the city. It was also more or less commonly acknowledged that, under the authority of the "ultimate decree" and on orders from the consul, citizens might be killed with impunity, if and as long as they presented an immediate danger to the state. This, of course, could not be said of the five men already in custody. The "decree of last resort," while proclaimed in time, could not justify their execution, because these men were not or no longer in arms and did not threaten the state with major disturbances. Riots from sympathizers or conspirators, however, were a possibility; it was the fear of such riots which made Cicero press for immediate punitive action. Naturally, he wanted the backing of the Senate and, thanks to Cato's firmness, he eventually received it—for what it was worth.

The consul's dilemma was that neither the "decree of last resort" nor the decree that made Catilina and his army public enemies justified the execution of the arrested Catilinarians. They were entitled to a trial according to the Sempronian law. Somewhat later, Publius Clodius did attack Cato as "hangman of citizens not convicted,"[4] but legally, responsibility rested with the consul who had put Cato's motion to the vote and had the five men executed.[5] He alone was accountable. Other attacks were justifiably directed not against Cato, but against Cicero, and they came soon enough, only a few weeks later, still in December.[6]

There was, in fact, no valid defense against the charge that the Sempronian law had been violated when the Catilinarians were executed. There is Cicero's own reaction to this in various speeches, first in those against Catilina (they were published soon after the events, and perhaps somewhat changed when a second edition was made in 60 B.C.),[7] then in the *pro Sulla* of 62, spoken in defense of a man accused of having been one of the conspirators, the *pro Flacco* of 59, and the *pro Sestio* of 56 B.C. Since all these testimonies were written somewhat after the actual events, they must reflect the well-meditated and, therefore, the strongest answer Cicero could find to the accusation that he had broken the law in having citizens executed without the people's consent. In three different passages (*pro Sulla* 32: *pro Flacco* 95; *pro Sestio* 11), he calls the five conspirators *hostes domestici*, public enemies, but of a specific and so far unheard of type—"domestic" enemies. More explicit is a passage in the fourth Catilinarian speech delivered in the Senate on that fateful 5 December, after Caesar had spoken, but before Cato's speech. Cicero's main intention was then to assure his peers that he, as consul, would obey whatever the vote of the Senate might be and that they should speak their minds, without regard for his, the consul's sake. (This, by the way, is as close as he comes to admitting that he, as consul, was ultimately responsible for what was then to happen.) In paragraph 10, he acknowledges that Caesar has reminded the house of the Sempronian law, but denies that the law was applicable. He said: "but whoever is an enemy of the republic cannot be a citizen under any circumstances."[8] It is absolutely correct that *civis* and *hostis*, citizen and enemy, are mutually exclusive. If the five were citizens, the Sempronian law applied and they could not legally be executed without a trial. If, however, they were enemies, they could be killed with impunity. The point is, of course, that Cicero's postulate that the five were enemies is unwarranted. No citizen became a *hostis* just by committing acts hostile to the state, unless the Senate formally declared him to be a *hostis* (as the *patres* had done with Catilina himself and those in his army). When proof came that the five conspirators had acted in a hostile manner, they were immediately arrested and there seemed to be no need of any such formal declaration by the Senate. Without it, however, they remained citizens and as such were protected by the Sempronian law—that is to say, entitled to a trial before a people's court.

Cicero understandably wanted to create the impression that what had taken place was the killing of public enemies, not the execution of citizens without a trial. For that purpose, he invented the term *hostes domestici* and argued that whoever had committed hostile acts was ipso facto a *hostis* or (to put it differently) if he had been a citizen, he thereby ceased to be one. None of that was true.[9] It was special pleading, an ad hoc construction intended to make people believe that the five had automatically lost their citizenship by what they had done (and confessed to). The people's court would have done no more than give its verdict, either "guilty" or "not guilty," whereas punishment was prescribed by law—execution for those found guilty of treason. Under the circumstances, the court might have been no more than a formality—but it was mandatory under the law. Cicero circumvented the law. Publius Lentulus, he said, had forfeited the right to be a praetor and a citizen. But Lentulus, after his confession, had to formally resign his praetorship, an act which proves that he was not considered to have automatically lost it.[10] By the same token, he could not have automatically lost his citizenship. In fact, he died a Roman citizen.

For these reasons, all those who were opposed to the executions continued to speak of the five conspirators as "citizens." So did Clodius when he attacked Cato; so did the new tribune Metellus Nepos a few weeks after the events, when he attacked Cicero; and so did Clodius again, with more success, in 58 B.C. By the same token, Cicero and all who sided with him continued to call these men "enemies." If Sallust can be trusted, it was Cato in his famous speech who helped Cicero find the rhetorical image of "domestic enemies" when he called the conspirators "enemies apprehended within the walls" ("intra moenia deprensi hostes").[11] However, still according to Sallust, Cato slipped in his motion and correctly called them citizens, if "most criminal citizens" ("sceleratissimi cives").[12]

Only a few days after their death, as soon as he had assumed office on 10 December 63 B.C., the tribune Quintus Metellus Nepos began attacking Cicero for having executed untried Roman citizens. He had been a lieutenant of Pompey (who was about to wrap up the war against King Mithridates—the old king had met his death while Cicero was still consul) and Metellus's main goal was to secure for Pompey the command against Catilina and the glory that might ensue. He was strongly supported by Julius Caesar, who was about to begin his year as praetor. When Metellus's bill in favor of Pompey was vetoed by Cato, another tribune, violence erupted; the Senate passed the "ultimate decree" and suspended both Metellus and Caesar. Metellus immediately departed for Pompey's headquarters, while Caesar gave in and succeeded in reconciling the Senate; he was reinstated. In its opposition to Metellus, the nobility had rallied behind Cicero. The Senate even went beyond the immediate occasion and passed a motion that whoever should in the future demand the punishment of those responsible for the execution of the Catilinarians would be considered a public enemy.[13] The danger of revolution and civil war had not only united the Senate, but also caused the equestrian order to demonstrate solidarity. The House seemed, once again, firmly on top of events. It had rebuffed the tribune Metellus, disciplined the praetor Caesar, and denied Pompey his wishes (Pompey now paid the price for the rude way he treated Lucius Licinius Lucullus some years earlier when he took over the command in the East from him). All of this was the result of Catilina's machinations and of Cicero's counterattacks.

Cicero felt not only strong and safe, but indispensable.[14] He was now convinced he was the first and foremost statesman of Rome, that he deserved and could not fail to remain in this role. He had indicated earlier that he would not follow the custom of governing a province for another year after the consulship. Rome was where the action was and where, therefore, Cicero belonged. He barely acknowledged Pompey as his equal. This would not have mattered, had he only kept his opinion to himself. But being the man he was, he had to advertise it openly. In the third of the Catilinarian speeches, he said: "I know . . . that at one time in this state there have been two men, one of whom fixed the borders of your empire not by limits of the earth, but by the limits of the sky, the other preserved the home and abiding-place of this empire."[15] These words were addressed to the citizens of Rome, but he also wrote a letter directly to Pompey. Now, Pompey was already annoyed that Cicero had removed the obstacles that had long prohibited the triumph of Lucullus, Pompey's predecessor in the East and his enemy, and that his energy had thwarted Pompey's hope to play the major role in destroying Catilina and his followers.

Pompey's answer is lost (as is Cicero's letter); that it must have been very cold can be seen from Cicero's reaction, a second letter written in April of 62 B.C., which reads:

My achievements have been such that I did expect some congratulatory reference to them in your letter, in consideration not only of our intimacy, but of their importance to the state; and I can only suppose that you omitted any such reference because you were afraid of wounding anybody's feelings. Anyhow, you must allow me to say that what I accomplished for the salvation of our country is now approved by the deliberate pronouncement of the whole world; and when you return home, you will recognize that the wisdom as well as the courage I showed in my achievements was such, that you, though a much greater man than Africanus ever was, will find no difficulty in admitting me, who am not much less a man than Laelius, into close association with yourself both in public policy and in private friendship.[16]

While the wording, taken at face value, seems to indicate that Cicero conceded Pompey's precedence, it hardly conceals what he really meant: that Pompey could at best claim to be his equal. If Pompey were superior in warfare, so was Cicero in handling affairs of state. In sending a long memoir to Pompey and speaking about himself and their mutual relationship in the manner in which he did, Cicero offered Pompey, whose return to Rome was imminent, a partnership. He made no secret of his opinion that they both had reached a level well above all others. To Pompey, this was nothing but insolent presumption; to Cicero's dismay, he remained very cool for some time, until he realized that, for his own good, he needed whatever allies he could find. This happened two years later, when the Senate's protracted opposition to his requests had rendered him helpless; he was then finally prepared to publicly acknowledge that Cicero had his merits. Cicero immediately transmitted the welcome news to Atticus: "I brought Pompey, who had kept his own counsel about my achievements too long, into such a frame of mind that he assigned to me in the Senate, not once but often and at length, the credit of having saved our empire and the world"; and: "You may be interested to learn that he eulogizes my achievements . . . in far more glowing terms than his own, acknowledging himself as a good servant of the state but me as its savior."[17] First Pompey, then Pompey and Caesar, were the figures with whom Cicero liked to compare himself. He wrote to Atticus in the spring of 59 B.C., when Pompey had damaged his reputation by his alliance with the consul Caesar and his support of Caesar's highly controversial laws: "I used to be piqued by the thought that a thousand years hence Sampsiceramus's [Pompey's] services to Rome might be rated higher than mine. I can now rest easy on *that* score."[18] Almost a decade later, after Caesar had conquered Gaul and gone to war against the Republic, Cicero mentions the two protagonists, Pompey and Caesar, only to continue: "I do not rate the achievements of these great warlords above my own."[19] While the wording indicates that others might disagree, the essential point is Cicero's untroubled conviction that his own achievements surpass the glorious deeds of the two generals, and that therefore he had a much better claim than either of them to be the leader of the state.

It follows that Cicero was less than sincere when he later wrote that after the consulship, his aim was no more than "the dignified deliverance of my opinions in the Senate, and an independent position in dealing with public affairs."[20] In fact, he always wanted much more and this was no secret, certainly not for Atticus. Further proof is at hand if needed: One of the consuls always acted as president of the Senate. He reported on the issues he wished to have discussed, then called on the members, according to their rank, for their opinions. Former consuls *(viri consulares)* were asked first, but within this group, the consul who presided in January was at liberty to choose on whom to call first, second, third, and so on. This order then remained the same for the rest of the year. The higher one was on the list, the greater the honor.[21] On 1 January 62 B.C., soon after the crushing of the conspiracy, Cicero was *primus rogatus,* called upon first, with Catulus second, Lucullus third, Hortensius fourth (Pompey was still absent and did not attend until after his triumph in September of 61). The consul of 61, however, called first upon a kinsman, Gaius Piso (cos. 67) and only second upon Cicero. Although Cicero was still ahead of Catulus (cos. 78), Hortensius (cos. 69), and many others who were his seniors, he was offended and chose to interpret the slight as proof of the consul's "petty and perverse mentality." If he can be believed, the House itself showed its disapproval by booing, *admurmurante senatu*.[22] There can be no doubt: Cicero yearned to be recognized as first among his peers.[23]

Not that such pretension was much of a secret. Cicero was, in fact, accused more than once in these years of monarchic posture. A young noble, Manlius Torquatus, who had been on cordial terms with Cicero, but who in 62 was pressing for Publius Sulla's conviction as one of the conspirators, became so outraged at Cicero for defending Sulla that he called him another "foreign tyrant," *peregrinus rex* (like the Etruscan kings of the past). He also charged that Cicero was about to make the Republic into his kingdom. A year later, in 61 B.C., Publius Clodius cried out: "How long are we going to put up with this King?"[24]

Attacks such as these must reflect a good deal of reality—in the years that followed his consulship Cicero not only claimed but also performed the role of a political leader.[25] Cicero aspired no less than to be, and to remain, the leader, that *rei publicae rector,* that he would later portray in the beginning of the sixth book of his *De re publica*. Several passages make it quite clear that he saw himself in that role, for instance *De legibus* 3.14, where as a participant in the dialogue he reasons as follows: "For we can mention the names of many great practical statesmen who have been moderately learned, and also of many learned men who have had some little experience in practical politics; but who can readily be found, except this man [Demetrius of Phalerum, once regent of Athens], that excelled in both careers, so as to be foremost [*princeps*] both in the pursuit of learning and in the actual government of a State?" To which he makes Atticus reply: "Such a man can be found, I believe; in fact, I think he would be one of us three! But continue with what you were saying." Also in a letter to Atticus, written in December 50 B.C., just before the beginning of the Civil War: "In fact if that notion of a triumph . . . had not been put into my head, you really would not have much cause to desiderate the ideal sketched in my sixth volume."[26] With the Catilinarian affair, Cicero had become a symbol for optimatic firmness and when Catulus died in 61 or 60, there was, for some time, no one else willing to provide continuous leadership. Catulus's death, however, also deprived Cicero of a staunch supporter: "But I should like you to realize [he wrote to Atticus in May 60] that since Catulus died I have been holding to this optimate road without supporters or companions."[27]

There were, from his point of view, more and more disquieting symptoms that the political barometer was falling. There was, in 61, the scandalous acquittal of Clodius in a charge of sacrilege committed in 62 which involved Caesar's wife. It was the result of massive bribery and came as a heavy blow to all conservative circles. What was even worse for Cicero: during the affair, as a witness, he provoked the accused to such a degree that Clodius became his archenemy. He had hinted that Clodius had committed incest with his sister, the famous Clodia, who, even without her brother, was never short of lovers. Moreover, a new rift opened between the Senate and the equestrian order just at the time Cicero was convinced he had mended fences through his statesmanship during the Catilinarian crisis, when, in fact, the two orders had acted in solidarity to protect the Republic. This *concordia ordinum,* of which he was so proud, had been the temporary result of converging interests; it now broke up when interests once more diverged. Such was the case, for instance, in the matter of those knights (the *publicani*) who had licensed from the State the collection of taxes in Asia. Through miscalculation, they had incurred a heavy loss and wished their contract with the state amended, but had run into opposition by the Senate—Cato judged their request downright immoral.[28] In another case, the Senate treated Pompey, once he dismissed his army in the fall of 62, in a high-handed manner, by refusing to comply with his legitimate demands. These were the ratification of his political arrangements in the East and allotment of land for his veterans. In both instances, Cicero was more flexible, since he saw the danger of alienating the knights, Pompey, and the army. But he was unable to convince his peers that obstruction would be self-defeating. This, then, indicates sound political judgment but also that his political leverage was much weaker than it might seem.

Cicero was not blind to the various dangers that threatened the continuity of optimatic rule. He saw them more clearly and was more concerned about them than most others. In those years, he often expressed anxiety. And yet, as long as the potentially dangerous elements did not make common cause, the course that he was steering might continue for some time without major deviation. And while he voiced fear and concern, he also, now and then, voiced elation that he was at the helm. In such moments, Cicero was convinced that he could control everything and everyone. His megalomania bordered on the ridiculous. In June 60 B.C., he replied to a warning from Atticus concerning Pompey. This letter was written when Caesar was about to be elected consul, just a few months before the secret arrangement with Pompey and Crassus known as the "first triumvirate," a conspiracy which demonstrated how fragile the rule of the optimatic clique really was. In this letter, Cicero says, with regard to Pompey, that he has provided against the danger of dissension that would inevitably lead to major political conflicts. He continues: "that does not mean that I have abandoned my own constitutionalist policy, but that he has become more constitutionally minded and less inclined to court popularity with the masses at the expense of principle."[29] Now steaming at full speed, he continues with Caesar: "Supposing I manage to make Caesar, who is riding on the crest of the wave just now, a better citizen, am I harming the state so very much?"[30] In other words, Cicero is confident that he can guide (and improve) both Pompey and Caesar for the benefit of the state.

Several months later, everything had fallen apart. Pompey, Crassus, and Caesar had agreed to further each other's interests and to do nothing against the interests of each of them. Caesar, as consul, would introduce legislation to satisfy the demands of his partners: that Pompey's veterans be settled and his arrangements in the East be finally ratified; also that the *publicani*, for whom Crassus acted as spokesman and lobbyist, be granted the amendment to their contract. In return, the two would support Caesar's wish to secure more than the usual annual governorship of a province—a wish that would eventually lead to the conquest of Gaul, the Civil War, and Pompey's defeat and death.

The coalition of the three (or *Trikaranos,* the Three-headed monster, as Varro called it, borrowing a title from the Greek historian Theopompus)[31] was an extraconstitutional alliance, which immediately proved much more powerful than anything the oligarchy could muster. The first few months of Caesar's year as consul (59 B.C.) were turbulent. Caesar began by introducing an agrarian bill primarily to satisfy Pompey. He did so in the usual way by having it discussed in the Senate. The unyielding attitude of the optimates, led by the other consul, Calpurnius Bibulus, made Caesar change his strategy: he no longer cared for the House. He brought the bill directly to the people and crushed all opposition by violent means. Other bills then passed with less turmoil. Pompey's arrangements, made after the Mithridatic War, were ratified and the *publicani* finally received their rebate (both Crassus and Caesar personally profited greatly from this). The other consul, Bibulus, swept from the forum by violence, stayed at home for the rest of the year, passively and ineffectively resisting the rulers by publishing biting, and popular, edicts.

By April 59, the battle was over; the three men were in almost complete control. Cicero stayed away from the Senate; what he might say, or whether he would attend the meetings, no longer mattered. The man who had claimed that he would guide both Pompey and Caesar had been unable to put up more than verbal resistance. It was now obvious to him that he lacked any real power base, such as, for instance, a fortune that could buy all kinds of services or a gang of ruffians. He wrote to Atticus: "I had long grown tired of playing skipper, even when that was in my power. Now, when I have—not abandoned the helm, but had it snatched out of my hands and am forced to leave the ship, I want to watch the shipwreck they are making from *terra firma.*"[32]

That, however, was far from imminent. For the time being, the one shipwrecked was Cicero himself. He could have played it safe. Caesar had approached him several weeks before entering the consulship and asked for his support. This is certainly proof that he valued Cicero's abilities. Now, Caesar had always stood for that *popularis levitas* which Cicero detested. Moreover, Cicero had just published his epic about his year as consul, *De consulatu suo,* in which he had solemnly vowed to remain faithful to his course and to the cause of all "the decent" (*boni*).[33] He simply had to decline Caesar's offer. With the same epic, moreover, he had heavily offended Pompey, mainly with the unfortunate verse that could only be understood as an attempt to compare him unfavorably with Cicero: "May the weapons yield before the toga and the laurel give way before the language" ("cedant arma togae, concedat laurea linguae").[34] Not content to have made an enemy of Clodius, turned down Caesar, and offended Pompey, Cicero also alienated the *boni*. At least, they were not eager to invite him to join them in their struggle against the *triumviri*. Their reluctance had two reasons: first, he had long courted Pompey, whom they opposed and mistrusted; second, Cicero had irritated them for some time with his bragging and now, with his epic, more than ever before. In short, when Caesar assumed office, Cicero found himself completely isolated. As early as May 59, long before his exile, he complained for the first time about the ingratitude of the other leaders.[35]

He should have waited quietly for better times to come, but this was not in Cicero's nature. Instead, he complained publicly about the conditions of the day, that is to say, about the dominance of the three rulers. He did so in March, when he spoke for the defense at the trial of his former colleague as consul, Gaius Antonius (who was convicted anyway). While Cicero spoke without enthusiasm for Antonius, he seemed much more inspired in his criticism of the *triumviri*. They made him pay by letting Clodius loose against him. Caesar reacted swiftly: as *pontifex maximus*, he had, almost within the hour, removed the obstacles that so far had prevented the transition of Publius Clodius to the plebs. Clodius was a patrician, a Claudius, who had changed his name to the proletarian Clodius in order to win favor with the crowd.[36] That very day, with Pompey's assistance, Clodius was adopted as son by a member of the plebs half his age. As plebeian, he was now qualified to compete for the tribunate, a position that would give him innumerable possibilities for political activity. Cicero had long known his intention and long been afraid of this happening and of its consequences.He had turned Clodius into an implacable enemy in the trial that followed the religious scandal in which Clodius was involved, when he acted as a severe and caustic witness for the prosecution.[37] A few months after his adoption, Clodius was elected to be tribune in 58 and Cicero, still desperately trying to convince Atticus and himself that he had nothing to fear, nevertheless knew that he would have to brace himself against the coming storm.[38] He could not foresee, however, how severe that storm would be and how badly it would hurt him.

In 58 B.C., just as Lucius Calpurnius Piso, Caesar's father-in-law, and Aulus Gabinius, a partisan of Pompey, assumed their duties as consuls, Clodius introduced a bill that those who had executed untried citizens be outlawed, "qui cives indemnatos necavissent."[39] Although no name was mentioned, everyone knew this was aimed at Cicero. The wording was such that it applied, in a highly irregular manner, not only to future but also to past events. Cicero's expectation that Pompey, the whole Senate, the consuls, the knights, and the entire population of Rome would rally to his defense vanished in a few weeks. First, Cato, who could be expected to fight for him (or for the cause), was removed from Rome under pretext: a bill of Clodius commissioned him to organize Cyprus as a Roman province. Second, bribery (as with the consuls) and intimidation through violent gangs of those prepared to defend Cicero did their work.[40] The *nemesis* of 5 December 63 B.C. now caught up with him. The bill passed on 20 March 58. Cicero could have waited to see whether he would be indicted and, in that case, could have stood trial. Instead, he felt deserted and lost heart; he left the city on the eve of the vote. Clodius interpreted this as a confession of guilt and, in a new bill, demanded that Cicero be outlawed and that whoever tried to help him be punished.[41] This also passed among threats of violence and Cicero was now forced to leave Italy, since Clodius's second law had fixed the boundary within which he could be killed with impunity at a distance of 400 miles from Rome.

The "father of his country" had become an outlaw, a criminal without a country, since he had also lost his citizenship.[42] It is ironic that the same events on which Cicero's unique distinction rested were also the cause of his expulsion. A further irony is this: while he had condemned others without granting them the trial to which they, as citizens, were entitled (he interpreted the confession as sufficient proof of guilt), he himself was now condemned without the trial to which he was entitled (as Clodius interpreted his departure as sufficient proof of his guilt). If Cicero had broken the law, so had Clodius with his second bill, because it was a *privilegium*, not a general law, but a law *ad hominem*, aimed at a single individual, and, as such, invalid according to the legal standards of the Romans. Several senators, therefore, always regarded this second bill as illegal.[43] However, the question of law did not matter: politics had defeated law in the case of the Catilinarians and now once again in Cicero's case. The main difference was that the decision reached in 63 was irreversible, and that of 58 was not, although Clodius did his utmost to make it so.

Nevertheless, efforts to bring about Cicero's reinstatement and return began almost immediately. Already on 1 June 58, the majority of the Senate voted in that sense. It took, however, more than a year of maneuvering, legal debate, obstruction, and violence until the Senate voted 416 to one in favor of Cicero's return (Clodius cast the single opposing vote) and had the assembly accept the appropriate proposal (August 57 B.C.).[44]

Cicero spent the first six months of his exile in Salonica, the last nine in Durazzo. More than two dozen letters to Atticus survive from this time (the entire third book of the correspondence). They demonstrate the full measure of his depression and show, as D. R. Shackleton Bailey put it, "a Roman Consular without his toga."[45] Their tenor is as follows: no one else has ever suffered such a calamity.[46] Cicero is sick of life[47] and repeatedly alludes to suicide as the honest or proper way out.[48] While writing, he burst into tears, his grief grows from day to day and is about to overwhelm him.[49] Atticus, he says, is quite wrong to rebuke him for his dejection.[50] Yes, he himself has contributed to his predicament; he has made errors and lacked in courage and determination.[51] But the main fault lies with others: those whom he regarded as his friends have let him down; those whom he trusted have betrayed him—Hortensius first of all,[52] their motive being envy.[53] No, he never included Cato among those false friends.[54] Atticus, however, is not entirely without blame; he ought to have given better advice and could now do more than he does for Cicero's rehabilitation.[55] And Cicero says time and again that all is now lost and no hope is left[56]—only to immediately spur Atticus into fresh action on his behalf.

It is easy to pass sentence on Cicero for this unmanly behavior and unjust accusations of others, and he has often been condemned for them, from his own days to ours. Justified as these verdicts are, one must also bear in mind that Cicero was a man of extremes, in elation as well as in dejection. As a younger contemporary, Asinius Pollio, later said of him: "Would that he could have shown more temperateness in prosperity, more stoutness in adversity!"[57] Cicero perceived more strongly than others the effects of the good and the bad things that affect people. Moreover, these letters were written by a man who had suffered a terrible fall and a devastating blow to his ego. They were written on the spur of the moment and addressed to the person closest to him. They were not meant to be seen and analyzed by others. The great historian Barthold Georg Niebuhr, in the early nineteenth century, went so far as to condemn the practice of publishing letters "which reveal the inmost of an extraordinary human being, since it is neither right nor just to expose a single soul naked while most others are not."[58]

The historian, however, cannot afford to be that noble. He must, of course, use sources like these and he will often find them more informative and more trustworthy than others in which every word is carefully considered. What is, however, uncalled for is disrespect or contempt for those exposed in such a way to his professional curiosity. Furthermore, if Cicero is to be blamed for the weakness he revealed during this ebb in his fortunes, he deserves admiration for the way he rose again. He deserves credit for something else: Caesar, who wanted to neutralize but not necessarily to punish him, had offered Cicero a position in 59 B.C. that would have made him invulnerable. Cicero declined and did so at a time when he already knew that Clodius was to become a major threat.[59] In declining the offer, he kept his integrity,[60] but paid the price with his exile. Since Cicero the politician is under review, it is obvious that to turn down Caesar's offer was a political mistake.

And his exile has to be judged a complete failure. On the other hand, it resulted from a stand that makes Cicero the man gain what Cicero the politician loses. In the events of his last year, the opposite occurred: what Cicero the politician eventually gained diminished his human qualities.

Cicero always interpreted his exile as a tragedy that had befallen not only himself but also the state. This reflects his conviction that he and the Republic, once he had rescued it, were inseparable, and, in fact, one and the same.[61] It followed naturally that as soon as he was fully reinstated, he convinced himself that it was again his destiny to lead. He savored a triumphant return through Italy and arrived in Rome on 4 September 57 B.C. The ovations he received only strengthened such conviction. The situation at that time was as follows: Pompey, while still an ally of both Caesar and Crassus, had become jealous of Caesar's growing reputation (the second year of Caesar's campaigns in Gaul was coming to a close). He wanted another major position. The optimates, opposed to all three "rulers," refused. Cicero's natural place would have been with them, all the more since many of them had worked very hard for his return. Instead, Cicero sided with Pompey in a spectacular way and he did so in spite of the fact that he continued to be opposed to the dominance of the *triumvirs*. His move cost him the goodwill of the nobility without profiting him much. It was, indeed, a very strange decision, especially since Cicero knew very well that Pompey, on whose protection he had counted, had deserted him in his hour of danger.[62] It is true that Pompey later had contributed to Cicero's return, but at a time when that seemed likely anyway; his later activity could hardly obliterate his former shameful conduct. Nevertheless, Cicero decided to show gratitude for recent events rather than resentment of the past. On the other hand, he remained resentful of certain optimates, those "false friends" who had betrayed him. His support for Pompey may be explained in part as an attempt to get even with them. Even stronger must have been his determination to signal that he was back not as a pardoned man, but as a leader. When the Senate debated Pompey's wish to be entrusted with the provision of grain, the optimates expected Cicero to stay away from the proceedings.

Instead, he not only attended but moved that Pompey be given an extraordinary commission and major powers for five years to that end. This happened only a few days after his return from exile.[63]

The move did not please Caesar or Crassus; Pompey himself was not particularly grateful to Cicero, since he would have succeeded without him just as well. By now, signs of tension among the three rulers were quite obvious. As an old rift between Pompey and Crassus (exploited and aggravated by Clodius) widened, relations between Pompey and Caesar became uneasy. A tribune from among Pompey's followers was the first to indicate that soon there would be an attack on the legislation which Caesar had pushed through as consul in 59 and that the principal target would be his second agrarian bill which affected the so-called *ager Campanus*.[64] Cicero, who certainly wanted it known that he was close to Pompey, saw fit, in March 56, to attack Publius Vatinius, the author of the famous *lex Vatinia* of 59 on which Caesar's command in Gaul and Illyricum rested, extraordinary in its territorial extent and number of years. While still respectful of Caesar, he called Vatinius's bill a criminal act.[65] Moreover, when the question of the *ager Campanus* came up in the Senate on 5 April 56 B.C., Cicero once more felt that he should take the lead. He moved that the matter be seriously discussed on 15 May; the motion passed.[66] It was a threat, hardly veiled, to Caesar. Three years earlier, Pompey had supported Caesar's bill, but during a visit from Cicero just two days after the debate, he gave no indication that he was displeased with Cicero's activity or in any way concerned—nor did he bother to mention that he was on his way to meet Caesar. There can be no doubt that Cicero counted on his support for the attack on Caesar scheduled for 15 May. If it succeeded, the triumvirate would be destroyed. That would force Pompey to adopt the policy of the *boni*—men such as Cicero would finally be back at the helm.

The scheme turned out to be a miscalculation. Caesar at once sensed the danger and took swift action, which, in turn, proves that he felt seriously threatened.[67] He found a way to thwart the plans of his opposition. Within a few days, he was able to convince first Crassus (in Ravenna) and then Pompey or both men (at Luca) that common interests still bound them together.[68] The triumvirate was renewed; Pompey and Crassus would secure a second common consulship in 55 and receive extraordinary commands similar to Caesar's, whose own commission they undertook to have extended for another five years. The most prominent victim of the new alliance was the man who had stuck his neck out in order to destroy the old alliance, M. Tullius Cicero. He was thunderstruck and forced to retreat ignominiously.[69] He was so shaken that he went beyond neutrality: he became the spokesman of the three in the Senate and in the courts.

Chapter Four

"Good night to principle, sincerity, and honor!"

When the triumvirate was reactivated in April 56 B.C., Cicero realized at once that resistance against the three rulers would be as ineffective as it had been during Caesar's consulship in 59. Moreover, Pompey had made it quite clear that the three expected no opposition from him, even if he could not bring himself to offer support. While this seemed to indicate that they would be satisfied with Cicero's neutrality, Cicero felt (or pretended to feel) that, in fact, they wanted more. If so, wisdom suggested compliance. He decided, therefore, to support them and explained his decision by saying that he now had to think of his own safety.[1]

It is difficult to assess the sincerity of this statement. There was certainly an element of truth in his assertion that neutrality would be risky; it would leave him without protection (and Clodius remained a dangerous foe). In any event, it would have been very difficult for a senator of his rank and stature to steer a neutral course when all the others were willing to take sides. More to the point, perhaps, the idea of remaining inactive, silent, and inconspicuous did not appeal to him at all. But if he wanted to stay involved in politics, he had to give at least some support to those in power. He knew this meant that he would have to change his course somewhat, but he consoled himself by affirming that he was still aiming for the same port; in this sense he wrote to Lentulus Spinther, consul of 57 and now, in 56, governor of Cilicia, a member of the conservative establishment: "But just as in sailing it shows nautical skill to run before the wind in a gale, even if you fail thereby to make your port; whereas when you can get there just as well by slanting your yards, it is sheer folly to court disaster by keeping your original course, rather than change it and still reach your desired destination; on the same principle in the conduct of state affairs, while we should all have as our one aim and object what I have so repeatedly preached—the maintenance of peace with honor ["cum dignitate otium"]—it does not follow that we ought always to express ourselves in the same way, though we ought always to have in view the same goal."[2]

In the view of most observers, however, Cicero went much too far in adjusting his political course to the new conditions. As early as May 56 B.C. he moved in the Senate that certain requests of Caesar, which he himself only recently had labelled "monstrous," be granted. Furthermore, it was Cicero who had the motion passed that Caesar could have ten lieutenants (*legati*) and that the pay for two additional legions, which he had recruited without authorization, be charged to the state's budget.[3] A little later, none other than Cicero effectively opposed the efforts of some optimates to terminate Caesar's command in Gaul in the spring of 55 B.C.[4] He thereby demonstrated once more that as a politician he possessed all the skills necessary to reach important goals. At the same time, it was obvious that these goals were no longer his own and that he had ceased to be independent. The optimates accused him of desertion; to them he had just turned into another agent of the rulers.[5]

Almost from the beginning of his affiliation with the three rulers, Cicero had misgivings about his new position, but, at least for a while, he pretended to be completely at ease. Pompey was not the problem. Cicero had been close to him for years and was still grateful for his eventual intervention that made his return from exile possible. But he had always opposed the politics of both

Crassus and Caesar, which he felt now constrained to support. It was characteristic of him to blame others for what burdened his conscience.[6] It was all the fault of the optimates, who were still jealous of him, who had betrayed him in his predicament, who were very stingy in their estimates of the lost property and real estate to be restored to him. Moreover, they had evinced poor political strategy in constantly bullying Pompey, thus driving him into Caesar's arms, and in estranging the knights from the Senate. More than once, totally insensitive to Cicero's feelings, they had backed a criminal like Clodius, only because he was causing trouble for Pompey.[7] To top it all, they failed too often in their duties, spending more time at their fish ponds than at their responsibilities as leaders. Cicero once even went so far as to claim that they were now morally inferior to the triumvirs.[8] They had no reason to complain that Cicero had finally begun to think of his own safety and advantage.

But characteristically, such pretexts did not satisfy Cicero for very long. Whatever his faults, his conscience started bothering him whenever he slipped. He soon realized that he had done wrong and admitted as much to the person closest to him, Atticus. The speech on the consular provinces had foiled the attempt to have Caesar recalled from Gaul. No sooner had Cicero delivered it in the Senate than he was ashamed of it: "There was also the fact (I might as well stop nibbling at what has to be swallowed) that I was not exactly proud of my palinode. But good night to principle, sincerity, and honor!"[9] Ten months later, in April 55, when Pompey and Crassus were consuls, he confessed: "But as for me, reckoned a madman if I speak on politics as I ought, a slave if I say what is expedient, and a helpless captive if I say nothing—how am I to feel?"[10] Robin Seager has best described Cicero's conduct in these years after Luca: "Here Cicero may merit censure on various grounds, but it is hardly just to ignore the pressures that forced him to his palinode or the torment that its consequences so obviously brought to his conscience as well as to his pride."[11]

The principal service demanded of Cicero in the years from 56 to 54 B.C. was to defend in court a number of partisans of Caesar and Pompey.[12] At Caesar's request, he defended, together with

Pompey and Crassus, Caesar's agent, the Spaniard Cornelius Balbus, accused of having fraudulently obtained Roman citizenship. Pompey asked him to defend Caninius Gallus, who had been actively engaged in an attempt to obtain another major commission for Pompey in Egypt. Cicero also spoke for one of Pompey's former lieutenants, Aemilius Scaurus, indicted for exploitation of the province of Sardinia. While he could act as advocate in some of these trials without embarrassment, two other requests proved extremely hard for him to swallow. Caesar wanted him to defend Publius Vatinius, on whose bill rested Caesar's command in Gaul. Cicero had strongly attacked him in the days immediately preceding the conference at Luca, during his abortive attempt to destroy the coalition of the three. Pompey demanded the same service for Aulus Gabinius, who, in 67 B.C., had introduced legislation that gave Pompey the command against the pirates. But when Cicero in 58 B.C. had appealed to Gabinius, then consul, for protection against Clodius, he had met instead with hardly concealed hostility. The reason for that was that Clodius, to deprive Cicero of all possible support and to destroy him, had bribed Gabinius: he promised legislation that would give Gabinius a long-term governorship of the rich new province of Syria. Gabinius was now, in 54, finally returning from Syria.

Bowing to Caesar's request, Cicero agreed to defend Vatinius in court, but although Vatinius was acquitted, Cicero hardly enjoyed winning the case. Others openly showed their dissatisfaction. The consul of 57, Lentulus Spinther, who had done more than almost anyone to achieve Cicero's return from exile, wrote him from his province Cilicia that he could accept the fact that Cicero was reconciled to Caesar, but not that he defended Vatinius (nor that he was reconciled to Crassus).[13] Worse, though, was still to come. When Gabinius returned in the fall of 54 B.C., he was immediately indicted by a number of people and charged with various criminal offenses.[14] Cicero's inclination was to be one of the prosecutors. Pressure from Pompey precluded that, but Pompey wanted more than neutrality: "Pompey is putting a lot of pressure on me for a reconciliation, but so far he has got nowhere, nor ever will if I keep a scrap of personal independence."[15] At the first trial, on 23 October, Cicero appeared only as a witness. He was dismayed by Gabinius's acquittal, but remained confident that he would fall in one of the following trials. And so he did in December, despite full support from Pompey, despite written testimony from Caesar in his favor—and despite the fact that Cicero was defending him. Cicero had succumbed to the pressure. "The defence of Gabinius was the final humiliation, the negation of everything he had stood for."[16] It was during these months that the well-known defamatory pamphlet was circulated which depicted Cicero as an unscrupulous weathervane and which, in its final words, called him a "despicable deserter," *levissime transfuga.*[17]

Cicero was fully aware of his situation. He felt the contempt shown to him by his peers and he was covered with shame. As he wrote to his brother, he was not allowed to prosecute his enemies, but forced to defend some of them; not only was he not free in his thoughts, but not even in his hate.[18] What in Christian Meier's view was always true of Cicero certainly holds true for this time: that as a politician, he was not on a par with his successes, his mental ability, and his political rank; in short, not equal to his destiny.[19] And though his services were of value to the men in power, he was not blind to the fact that the three, with or without him, could do whatever they wanted.[20]

And yet, despite his impotence and humiliation, he had enough strength and virtue left to enable him to remain productive, even creative. In 55 B.C., he had produced the very substantial treatise *De oratore* (a dialogue on the ideal speaker) and in 54, at the lowest ebb of his reputation, he was busy writing *De re publica,* his doctrine of the ideal state.[21] It is perhaps not too bold to think that indeed the agony of the free republic and his personal dejection acted as the catalyst to such a work. More important, thanks to such work, Cicero finally overcame his depression of spirits; in it, he found the means to pull himself together and to stand upright again.[22]

If Cicero suffered from not being master of his decisions, not everything else in these years was equally bleak. His relationship with Caesar developed in an unexpected and pleasant way, even to some degree of cordiality. Caesar knew how to charm people and with Cicero he spared no effort. He made Quintus Cicero one of his lieutenants and wrote warmly to Marcus about his performance; he was receptive to letters of recommendation written by Cicero in favor of young people looking for a position on Caesar's staff. He more than once complimented him on his writings and was more than willing to let Cicero—as so many others—borrow a substantial sum of money. Cicero eventually felt stimulated to compose a poem on Caesar's expedition to Britain. The task was not easy; he dropped the draft for a while, but in December 54, the final product was ready—fortunately, it is lost.[23] As for Crassus, although a formal reconciliation had taken place at the urging of both Caesar and Pompey, Cicero continued to heartily dislike the man and did not hide his feelings in letters to trustworthy correspondents.[24] Crassus left Rome in November 55, not to return, since he was killed eighteen months later in a disastrous war against the Parthians. His son Publius, who had been a lieutenant of Caesar and was fond of Cicero, died with him; Cicero, upon nomination by Pompey and Hortensius, now became the young man's successor as *augur,* after some competition from Marcus Antonius, who was elected a few years later to that distinguished body. Crassus's death destroyed the triumvirate, at least in a formal sense; moreover, the personal bond between Pompey and Caesar weakened when Caesar's daughter Julia, happily married to Pompey, died in September 54 B.C. For some time, however, the two men remained on good or correct terms, Caesar still busy completing his conquest of Gaul, Pompey increasingly engaged in major affairs at home.

At Rome, a series of political scandals and major crises came to a head in January 52 when Clodius, for years the leader of a violent gang, got killed in a scuffle with the gang of his foe Milo. Widespread violence ensued, and the Senate building was burned down. Finally, Pompey was appointed consul without a colleague (only another name to avoid the title of *dictator* that Sulla had made odious), since he alone seemed capable of putting an end to what had become anarchy. He had long yearned for such a position, and mainly for that reason was opposed to Milo, since Milo was a candidate for the consulship (and the oligarchy's candidate).

If elected, Milo would be a strong consul, and there might not be a need for Pompey's services. Pompey acted swiftly to restore law and order and to eliminate Milo as a potential rival. At once, he introduced a new bill *de vi* (on violence) specifically tailored to deal with Milo. For that very reason, the bill was attacked as unconstitutional (a *privilegium*), but Pompey pushed it through.

Early in April, Milo stood trial for the murder of Clodius. Conditions were highly irregular: there was the new law of dubious legality and there was a large and hostile public. Clodius's adherents and large numbers of the mob with whom he had been popular thronged the forum, kept in check by military units which Pompey had posted as a safeguard against major disturbances. Under the new law, pleading was drastically limited; the defense was allowed to speak for only three hours. Because of that, only Cicero spoke for the defendant. In the most adverse circumstances, he loyally stood by the man who had often supported and protected him. Late and unfriendly sources recount the familiar story that Cicero was so intimidated by the heckling of the crowd and the presence of the soldiers that he spoke very tentatively and very briefly, and that he did not finish his speech.[25] The truth is, however, that he endured. The speech was stenographed and was still being read more than a century later by Asconius and Quintilian. Asconius, whose model commentary on both the trial and the much more refined speech which Cicero later published survives, says only that Cicero spoke "with less than his customary resolution" ("non ea qua solitus erat constantia"). Under the circumstances, with witnesses having testified to Milo's intention to kill, in the middle of a hostile crowd and knowing that Pompey wanted Milo condemned, Cicero displayed great courage.[26] While it was to no avail in the end, he had shown spirit and demonstrated that he still was something more than the puppet of the rulers.

He followed the same course in other trials stemming from the violent events of January. He defended Milo's lieutenant Marcus Saufeius against charges connected with Saufeius's role in the murder of Clodius; he successfully defended him not once, but twice, since after the first trial, held according to Pompey's new law on violence, and his acquittal, Saufeius was again indicted under an older one, the *lex Plautia de vi*. Furthermore, on 9 December 52, when the tribunate of Titus Munatius Plancus Byrsa, who had been a close associate of Clodius, ended, Cicero took him to task for his part in the riots and in the burning of the Curia following Clodius's death. So, almost twenty years after prosecuting Verres, Cicero once again prosecuted in court. He won despite Pompey's efforts to have the accused spared and he savored his triumph.[27] Cicero, it seems, had served notice—he was determined to be his own man again.

Soon thereafter, however, and much against his will, Cicero had to leave Rome to govern one of the provinces. Twice before he had excused himself from such obligation, in the years following his praetorship (65 B.C.) and his consulship (62 B.C.). This time, however, he had no choice but to obey a recent law of Pompey which had placed a mandatory interval for praetors between their year of office in Rome and a provincial command.[28] The intention was to curb the corruption and greed of those in office. As a consequence, there was a shortage of men eligible for governorships, and those who had held a higher magistrature in an earlier year, but had not thereafter governed a province, were now sent out to such posts. Cilicia, at the border of Asia Minor and Syria, fell to Cicero. He left Rome on 1 May 51 B.C., arrived in his province on 31 July, and left it exactly one year later on 30 July 50 B.C., on the very first day the law permitted. During all that time, two eventualities gave him nightmares: that the Parthians might attack and that his term might be extended for another year. Luckily enough, he was spared both.

Since in Cilicia Cicero was an administrator and a judge rather than an active politician, his performance as governor need not be discussed. Suffice it to say, he took as his model his former teacher Mucius Scaevola during his celebrated governance of Asia. His letters from that year (over a hundred, if those addressed to him are included) are very instructive. They illustrate Roman provincial administration in general, and Cicero's standards and daily routine as a *proconsul* in particular. It is generally agreed that he governed with more concern for his subjects and with greater justice and humanity than most Roman governors of the time. This judgment, however, is often qualified by statements such as, "Cicero is all the time thinking, not of the welfare of Cilicia, but of his own reputation."[29] In fact, he was concerned with both and the province fared much better under him than ever before, and better than most other provinces under their governors.

Before leaving Rome, Cicero had made sure he would be kept informed of major political developments. A former student, later a client of his, Marcus Caelius Rufus, promised to send him regular reports, twelve of which survive.[30] He was well placed for such a task; he had been tribune in 52 and was aedile in 50 B.C., a gifted and frivolous young man who knew how to write elegantly and who, for some time, as a lover of Clodia, had been Catullus's successful rival.[31] His letters to Cicero provide the most informative contemporary evidence about the politicking which eventually led to the breakup between the optimates and Pompey on the one side, and Caesar on the other. This complicated and fascinating story cannot and need not be retold here,[32] since it developed without Cicero. When he returned to Italy late in November 50 B.C., matters had reached the point of war. In September, Caelius had already expressed the view that war seemed unavoidable and Cicero himself had written to Atticus in October, first from Ephesus, then from Athens, that it was likely.[33]

In the spring of 51 B.C., the consul Marcus Marcellus made the first serious move to terminate Caesar's command in Gaul. This was several months after the fall of Alesia and the capture of Vercingetorix; it could be argued that Gaul had been effectively subjugated. Nothing came of it, but the question remained on the agenda of the optimates. About a year later, it became obvious that Pompey had moved away from Caesar and had formed close ties with a group of influential nobles. He had remarried, his new wife being the daughter of Metellus Scipio, one of those conservatives who were determined to have Caesar resign his command, but were unwilling to let him go from there, without any interval, into a second consulship. By September 50, Cicero's correspondent Caelius was brooding seriously over the question of whose side to take in the coming war. Cicero began to ask himself that same question in October, when he received letters from Pompey and Caesar, each writing that he counted on his support.[34] The necessity to choose tormented him to the degree that he even wished he could have stayed in his province!

There was no doubt in his mind that the honest cause was represented by the leaders of the Senate and Pompey.[35] Caesar, on the other hand, seemed the stronger.[36] It was now too late to oppose him after he had gained such formidable strength.[37] As early as September, people speculated that if an armed conflict erupted, Pompey might abandon Rome.[38] Cicero's dilemma was worsened by the irksome fact that a substantial loan received from Caesar was not yet repaid. True, Cicero had urged Atticus to arrange for repayment before he left for his province,[39] but for some reason, he still owed Caesar the money a few days before the Civil War began.[40] From the victory of either Caesar or Pompey, Cicero expected terror such as Rome had witnessed in the days of Marius, Cinna, and Sulla,[41] and he was convinced that victory from either side would mean the end of the Republic and autocratic rule of the victor.[42] "Victory will bring many evils in its train, including the certainty of a despot."[43] His conclusion was, "Peace is what is needed," "pace opus est."[44] He repeated what his mentor Scaevola had once said: "Even an unjust peace is better than the most just of wars against one's countrymen."[45] He worked for peace with all his energies, as soon as he returned from Cilicia, and even after hostilities began on 10 January 49 B.C. It was to no avail.

His young friend Caelius had by now joined Caesar's camp. A few months earlier, he had written to Cicero that, in the event of civil strife, one had to support the just cause; if, however, there were civil war, one must choose the stronger side. So he did, when the time came.[46] A principled man like Cicero was incapable of acting in such a cynical manner. He might bend under pressure and stretch his principles, but he would not flatly renounce them. If there were to be a war, he knew his place was in Pompey's camp; only once, terrified by Caesar's offensive thrust and the news that Pompey had abandoned Rome on 21 January, did he waver for a moment.[47] While he was willing to concede that Caesar might have some valid grievances, there was just no excuse for going to war against the government and his fellow citizens. Cicero clearly recognized that Caesar's whole case rested on the question of his personal dignity (*dignitas*),[48] and this is, in fact, the only reason which Caesar himself offers to justify his decision to go to war.[49] Whatever the merits of Caesar's cause might have been before, his decision to pursue it in civil war made it morally inferior. Pompey was justified in declaring that he regarded as an enemy anyone who did not join his ranks to defend the Republic, while Caesar had to be satisfied with requesting neutrality.[50] When he claimed all who were not against him as "his men," he, in fact, almost acknowledged the weakness of his cause.

As long as Pompey remained in Italy, Caesar courted no one more intensely than Cicero, for three full months; Cicero stood fast. He was still the holder of an *imperium* (from his governorship) and was now appointed commissioner for the recruiting in Campania. He was not very effective.[51] Major things preoccupied him: the appropriate strategy to use against Caesar's attack, and whether any hope of reconciliation still remained. His daily letters to Atticus are filled with strong criticism of what he considered Pompey's incompetence. The clearer it became that Pompey and the government would abandon Italy, the more agitated Cicero became, troubled about what he should do and what the right time for action was. His conscience told him to stay with Pompey and the forces of the Republic, for better or for worse; honesty demanded it, while caution seemed to point in the other direction.[52] Moreover, some hope remained that a compromise might be reached and peace restored. In that case, Cicero's services would be needed as those of a prominent statesman who had always stood against the hard-liners and hawks and always advocated peace. He thus had a valid and honest reason to hesitate, all the more since he was one of the few men acceptable to both sides as mediator. Once in Pompey's camp, he would lose such ability and all freedom of movement. Other factors almost certainly contributed to his hesitation: he was not made for war and desperately tried to stay out of it. When Pompey, late in February, summoned him, Cicero wrote that he could not come because the enemy had already cut him off.[53]

While he pondered how to reconcile what was honest with what was advantageous, things had run their course. Pompey and his troops, besieged by Caesar in Brindisi, had escaped across the Adriatic to Greece on 17 March. Cicero was left behind. He immediately felt ashamed to have missed the boat.[54] And Caesar at once started to press harder. He told him that since he had not yet joined Pompey, there was no reason to do so after his flight. He wanted Cicero to come to Rome and support him in the Senate, which was convened for 1 April,[55] although most of the senators, at least those of the higher ranks, had gone with Pompey.

On 28 March, only ten days after Pompey's escape, Caesar visited Cicero at the latter's estate at Formiae. The conversation as described in Cicero's letter to Atticus of that same day was polite, but grim.[56] Cicero refused to come to Rome and to adorn the meeting of a rump Senate which, for him, had not the slightest appearance of legality. Caesar replied that Cicero's absence would be interpreted as a verdict against himself and urged Cicero to come and speak in favor of peace. Could Cicero speak as he pleased? Of course: Caesar would not even think of dictating to him what to say. Cicero then said that he would speak against continued military operations in Spain (where Pompey had an army) and Greece (where Pompey now was), and that he would speak well of Pompey. Caesar replied that he did not want any of that. Cicero kept his ground; it was a crucial moment. While he had shown signs of weakness for two months, he did not falter in this confrontation. Caesar was displeased. A little later, still worried that Cicero might join the opposition, he sent word that he forgave his absence from the Senate. The minimum Caesar expected, however, was neutrality and he sternly warned him not to leave Italy[57]—he would not even allow him to go to a small place such as Malta (Cicero had been thinking of that) to quietly await the outcome of the war.

Cicero, however, had had enough. Intense vexation finally helped him to resolve the issue; he prepared his escape. He discussed the matter with two other ex-consuls, whose villas were close to his own; he found both extremely faint-hearted,[58] but remained himself determined. He was somewhat delayed by dead calm, but eventually, on 7 June 49 B.C., he sailed away to Pompey's camp. From aboard the vessel, he sent a note to his wife, saying that he had left "to defend the republic together with my peers."[59]

This may have been his intention, but it was not exactly what he did after his arrival at the republican headquarters. Although some people judged him a coward for coming so late, he was well received because his rank and reputation added strength to the cause. Marcus Cato, however, said that he would have served their cause better by staying in Italy and trying to bring about mediation and peace.[60] Since Caesar just recently had expressed his wish for peace, Cicero now tackled Pompey, but found him strongly adverse to the idea of reconciliation.[61] Cicero, for his part, refused any responsibility (no position there, he said, suited his dignity) and, while he remained in camp, he went around criticizing the high command and getting on people's nerves with bitter jokes and gloomy forecasts.

When, after a while, Caesar's army completely blockaded Pompey's camp at Durazzo, Cicero received a letter from Publius Cornelius Dolabella, a patrician noble, who had recently become his son-in-law and happened to be one of Caesar's lieutenants. This letter,[62] written in May or June 48 B.C., pointed out that Pompey's situation was hopeless. Cicero should, therefore, think of his own best interests: "You have done enough for obligation and friendship; you have done enough for your party too and the form of commonwealth of which you approved. It is time now to take our stand where the commonwealth is actually in being rather than in following after its old image, to find ourselves in a political vacuum." Dolabella went on to recommend that Cicero retire to Athens or to any peaceful community he pleases; Caesar would be generous and he, Dolabella, would not fail in petitioning him for Cicero's sake.

This appeal had no immediate effect on Cicero. A little later, Pompey, in a brilliant attack, forced his way through the blockade.[63] While the theater of war shifted to Thessaly, Cicero, in poor health, remained in Durazzo where Cato had been put in charge of the town. On 9 August, Caesar defeated Pompey in the battle of Pharsalus. Without his army, Pompey fled to Egypt, where he was murdered on arrival. The republican fleet was still intact and the remaining forces gathered at its base in Corfu. Cato proposed that Cicero, as befitting his rank, be elected commander-in-chief. When Cicero declined, Pompey's son Gnaeus threatened his life, and Cato had to come to Cicero's rescue. Cicero, who saw no point in continuing the war, sailed to Patras. There he received another letter from Dolabella saying that Caesar wished Cicero to go to Italy as soon as possible.[64] After some deliberation, Cicero went, landing in Brindisi in October 48 B.C. He was to remain there for almost a year.

Within days of his arrival, it dawned on him that he had acted too hastily and had made the wrong decision. He soon learned about Pompey's death and that Caesar was in Alexandria. As long as Caesar had not decided Cicero's fate, Cicero was not allowed to leave Brindisi, where his old enemy, Publius Vatinius, was in charge (he, in fact, showed every kindness to Cicero, mindful, it seems, of Cicero's speech a few years ago, that had saved him from exile). Incoming news contributed to Cicero's depression. He learned that other men of his rank had retreated to places in Greece or to islands such as Samos or Lesbos, to await the end of the war. This, he realized, was what he should have done; it was much more dignified than his own haste, which gave the impression that he wanted Caesar's pardon at all costs. Moreover, Marcus Antonius, whom Caesar had left in charge of Italy, publicized the fact that Cicero was sitting and waiting at Brindisi, thus greatly embarrassing him, not because he meant to harm Cicero (at that time the two men were still on friendly terms), but because Caesar had sent him a written order not to allow prominent members of the opposition to come to Italy. Since Cicero was already there, it was necessary to issue a statement excepting him from that ruling. And while Caesar was caught in Egypt, entangled first with his enemies, then with Cleopatra, unable for months to extricate himself, no assurance came forward about Cicero's fate. On the other hand, Caesar's enemies, led by Metellus Scipio, consul of 52 B.C. and Pompey's father-in-law, and by Marcus Cato, had made Africa their base of resistance and had collected substantial forces, to which King Juba of Mauretania added his own. After all, far from being finished, the war would continue, with the possibility that Cicero might be treated as a deserter, should Caesar lose.[65] He could not share Atticus's optimism that peace with those in Africa could be negotiated.[66]

Familiar feelings of guilt and shame returned. Cicero admitted that he had nobody to blame but himself.[67] Moreover, he knew all too well that many people thought that his place ought to be with the party in Africa[68] and such a view was irrefutable. Finally, after ten miserable months, a reassuring letter came from Caesar (who, at that time, in August 47 B.C., was about to defeat Mithridates's son Pharnaces in Asia Minor).[69] In late September, Caesar was back in Italy, the two men met, and Cicero was treated with the utmost courtesy and respect. He was pardoned and free to leave. In October, he arrived in Rome. As he had predicted three years earlier, the Civil War had led to the rule of a monarch, under the title *dictator*. The two open questions were whether Caesar would remain victorious (the war was not over yet) and, if so, whether he would revive the Republic, as Sulla had done. The answers to these questions would decide whether or not there could be any future role in politics for Marcus Tullius Cicero.

Chapter Five

Liberty Recovered and Lost

After Caesar's return to Italy in September 47 B.C., nobody expected an immediate answer to the question of what form of government he would restore. As had been the case with Sulla, that would have to wait for the end of the war. Caesar made haste to end it. In December, he crossed over to Africa, and on 6 April 46 he decisively defeated the enemy at the battle of Thapsus. A few days later, Marcus Cato, who commanded Utica, took his own life. He knew that Caesar wanted above all to pardon him and he was all the more determined to foil his intention, since he held that Caesar had no right whatsoever either to kill or to pardon any Roman citizen: "I am unwilling to be under obligation to the tyrant for his illegal acts. And he acts illegally in saving, as if their master, those over whom he has no right at all to be the lord."[1] Caesar's acclaimed clemency is hereby defined as the pardon granted by a monarch to his subject; *clementia Caesaris* is, consequently, an indication that the Republic is dead.[2]

Much has been written about Caesar's famous clemency; and the late Andreas Alföldi has dedicated a book-length study to *clementia Caesaris,* the last major work he was able to complete.[3] While it seems just to praise Caesar in this respect, as Alföldi persuasively does, the fact nevertheless remains that none other than Caesar himself had brought about the circumstances under which scores of Roman citizens, through no fault of their own, became dependent on clemency.[4]

Peace seemed finally at hand in the summer when Caesar returned to Rome to celebrate four triumphs (for the victories in Gaul, Egypt, Asia Minor, and Africa). It was not to be. The sons of Pompey had occupied Spain and rallied a force of thirteen legions. In the fall, Caesar left again to deal with them. He defeated them in March 45 B.C. at Munda and returned to Italy that fall to celebrate another triumph. In February 44, he was made permanent dictator (*dictator perpetuus*) and a few weeks later, preparing to leave for a war against the Parthians, he was murdered. He had done nothing to restore a traditional constitution nor indicated that he had any such intention for the future. Civil war had, in fact, produced monarchy.

The final result had not always been taken for granted in the course of these years, not even by Cicero. While he had long predicted it, he nevertheless repeatedly expressed the hope that Caesar might restore some kind of constitutional government and that there might still be a political role to play for him and the likes of him. The news of Caesar's victory at Thapsus had just reached Rome, about 20 April 46 B.C., when Cicero addressed Terentius Varro, the famous scholar, who had been one of Pompey's lieutenants defeated by Caesar in Spain.[5] His advice to Varro was to lie low for the present and to concentrate on his literary studies. "We used to go to them only for pleasure, now we go for salvation. If anybody cares to call us in as architects or even as workmen to help build a commonwealth, we shall not say no, rather we shall hasten cheerfully to the task." A few months later, he wrote about Caesar to another friend as follows:[6] "Even if he were to will that the state be such as he perhaps desires and as all of us ought to pray for, there is nothing he can do. He has too many associates to whom he has tied himself." In the meantime, it had dawned on Cicero that his services would not be required, but he continued to have hopes for the state. There are similar statements in 46 B.C., down to October, for instance:[7] "In spite of all, I think I see a hope that . . . Caesar will try and is already trying, to get us some sort of a constitutional system."

The climax, during which hope almost changed to expectation, came in September 46 and is manifested in the speech *pro Marcello*. Cicero attended the Senate for some time (he had no choice), but had remained silent. When he broke his long silence, it was to thank Caesar for having yielded, quite unexpectedly, to the full Senate's dramatic request that one of Caesar's severest enemies be pardoned. This was Marcus Marcellus, who as consul in 51 had pressed for Caesar's discharge from his command in Gaul. He now lived in exile in Mytilene and was much too proud to ask for a pardon. Cicero was genuinely moved by the generosity of the act and warmly thanked Caesar for what he called the greatest testimony to his clemency. What makes the speech so important is the fact that he openly requests that Caesar restore some form of constitutional government.

> It is all these wounds of war's infliction which you are called upon to heal, and which none but you can treat. Consequently it was with regret that I listened to those famous and philosophic words of yours: "I have lived long enough either for nature or for glory." Long enough, perhaps, if you will have it so, for nature—and for glory too, if you like; but, what is more than all this, for your country all too brief a span. . . . So far are you from consummating your chiefest labours, that you have not yet laid the foundation of all your plans. . . . But if this, Gaius Caesar, was destined to be the issue of your mortal works, that, after subduing your adversaries, you should leave the state in the condition where it stands to-day, look to it, I beg of you, that your superhuman qualities win not admiration rather than glory. . . . This chapter, then, still awaits you; this act yet remains to be played, to this must you summon all your powers—to plant the constitution firmly.

This, Cicero concludes, Caesar still owed to his country; only after having brought that about could Caesar say that he had lived long enough.[8]

A few weeks later, Caesar left again to fight the war in Spain. Cicero became very doubtful that what he hoped for would ever come to pass. In January 45, he wrote to Gaius Toranius, one of the republicans still in exile: "I only hope we may one day enjoy

some form of settled constitution,"[9] and to another in similar circumstances, his friend Aulus Torquatus: "But if there is some hope
for our communal affairs, you must have your share in it, whatever
the nature of the settlement is to be."[10] By May 45, however, even
such vague hopes had vanished.

Under Caesar's dictatorship, there was no room for any political activity. No serious business was to be done in the Senate;[11]
everything was in the hands of a single man;[12] in his absence, two
individuals appointed by him, his intimate friends Balbus and Oppius, conducted all business in Caesar's name. They were not
elected magistrates and were accountable to no one except Caesar.[13] The condition of the state, as described by Cicero, was a
"departure from the law" ("a iure discessum est").[14] No significant
trials took place anymore; they had come to a halt when the Civil
War began. The last two preserved speeches of Cicero for defend-
ants are those for the Pompeian Quintus Ligarius and for King
Deiotarus of Galatia. They were, however, not delivered in a court
of law, but in Caesar's palace and in his presence, Caesar acting as
both prosecutor and sole judge.[15] Cicero had lost his forensic
kingdom.[16]

To him, two things remained that he could do with dignity:[17]
first, use his influence with several of Caesar's assistants to prepare
the ground so that more of those republicans who still lived in
exile could be pardoned, and keep their spirits up through en-
couraging letters;[18] second, as he had done before and had advised
Varro to do, fall back on literary work. During the years 46–44
B.C., while Cicero was forced into political inactivity, he composed
an amazing number of rhetorical and philosophical works, small
ones and big ones. This output has been marvelously assessed in
Klaus Bringmann's *Untersuchungen zum späten Cicero.*[19] Since all of
this work, however, was but a surrogate for politics, it need not be
discussed here, except for that portion which was also a political
manifesto. The first was *Brutus,* an account of the Roman orators
and their achievements. The book was also intended to justify Cicero's policy of mediation.[20] It was written in the winter of 47/46
B.C. and published in March 46, just before the news about Thapsus and the death of Cato became known. This news prompted

Cicero to write another treatise. For, more than anything else, Cato's suicide instilled in him the agonizing thought that he had already sinned in still being alive.[21] The least he could do (and better than anybody else) was to immortalize the man as the symbol of liberty and republicanism. He wrote *Cato,* a glowing tribute to the memory of the uncompromising and staunch advocate of law and tradition. The pamphlet was bound to be understood as an adverse judgment of Caesar. Cicero was aware of that and wrote to Atticus: "I cannot work anything out which your boon companions [he meant Balbus and Oppius] would read with equanimity, let alone enjoyment. Even if I were to keep clear of his speeches in the Senate and his whole political outlook and opinions and choose simply to praise his seriousness of purpose and steadfastness, even this would grate upon their ears. But no genuine eulogy of that remarkable man is possible without paying tribute to the way he foresaw our present situation and strove to avert it and abandoned his life rather than witness it in actuality."[22]

And indeed, Caesar felt challenged. After one of his lieutenants, Aulus Hirtius, wrote a polemical pamphlet about Cato, Caesar himself replied with *Anticato,* an angry treatise where he stooped to shabby polemics.[23] Others again reacted in favor of Cato: Marcus Brutus (Cato's nephew), Marcus Fabius Gallus, and Munatius Rufus.[24] Caesar treated his dead opponent very differently from his usual style; none other than Cicero attests that after Pompey's death, Caesar spoke of him only in honorable terms[25] and it is well known that he had Pompey's statue reinstated in the Senate House. The fact that he forgot himself when writing about Cato seems to indicate that he might have had a feeling of inferiority toward Cato which he did not have toward Pompey.[26] Cicero had stirred all that up with his *Cato.* That he wrote and published the piece at all (he even had it sent to Caesar) shows the same combination of loyalty, courage, and stubbornness that he could occasionally reveal, qualities which he had displayed in the defense of Milo in 52 B.C.

Verbal demonstrations, however, could not change reality. With the passage of time, Cicero's expectation that Caesar would restore a constitutional government faded away. In May 45, while Caesar was ending the Spanish War, Cicero felt that there was no hope left. Caesar, he learned, was quoted as having said "that he will not go to fight the Parthians until he has settled affairs here," but Cicero had nothing but sarcasm for this news: "For pity's sake let us chuck this nonsense, and be half free at any rate."[27] To Atticus, he wrote in August 45: "Indeed? Brutus reports that Caesar has joined the honest men? Good news! But where is he going to find them—unless he hangs himself?"[28]

Cicero's tone has become very bitter and, toward Caesar, extremely hostile. This development seems to be reflected in a change of vocabulary. While, as early as Caesar's consulship in 59 B.C., Cicero had spoken of Caesar's intention to rule and used expressions appropriate for kingship *(regnare, regnum)*,[29] he seems to have avoided them after the battle of Pharsalus. Instead, he used slightly more neutral and less offensive terms, such as *dominatus,* to indicate Caesar's dominating position.[30] It was only in the summer of 45 B.C., when he no longer had any illusion that Caesar might restore republican forms, that he called him *rex* downright and spoke of the games which Caesar was about to sponsor as "royal shows" *(munera regia).*[31] And while some of his earlier uses of "royal" terminology did not mean much more than excessive power or an intention of gaining such power, this time Cicero had in mind the real and odious meaning of kingship, that is to say, the absolute power of a monarch, with or without the royal title and the royal insignia.[32] Whether Caesar was called king, tyrant, or permanent dictator did not much matter; what mattered was that he ruled alone and wanted to rule permanently.

At the time that he began to call Caesar *rex,* in the summer of 45 B.C., Cicero also wrote to Atticus that there was a lack of such men as Servilius Ahala and Lucius Brutus, the two tyrannicides par excellence.[33] Brutus, of course, was the hero who had overthrown King Tarquinius Superbus and the monarchy; Servilius Ahala had murdered Spurius Maelius, a man suspected of aspiring to monarchic rule. Cicero's young friend Marcus Brutus happened to be a descendant of both these heroes (his mother was a Servilia). Brutus was a personal enemy of Pompey (who in 78 B.C. had treacherously executed his father). When the Civil War came, he subordinated his personal feelings to the cause and fought under

Pompey at Pharsalus. After the defeat, he accepted Caesar's pardon and favor. His mother Servilia, who, through her mother, was Cato's sister, was rumored to have had an affair with Caesar. Brutus must have been torn between conflicting loyalties. In 45 and 44, Cicero reminded him repeatedly, in treatises dedicated to him, of his predecessor's famous deed or that of the Athenian tyrannicides, Harmodius and Aristogiton.[34] Tradition had long synchronized these two events of circa 510 B.C. It seems beyond doubt that Caesar's assassination was on Cicero's mind by the summer of 45[35] and that he focused on Brutus. And the fact that (in Cicero's opinion) Caesar had become *rex* was undoubtedly why Cicero wished him dead.

The significance of the change in Cicero's mood, as far as the future of the Republic was concerned, from temperate optimism to despair, has been well observed. The late Hermann Strasburger[36] pointed out that the philosophical work written during Caesar's last year of life was not only a description of Greek philosophy, but also "a well planned attack on Caesar's rule."[37] He observed that Caesar's name is never mentioned in works later than the *Brutus* of spring 46, but published before Caesar's murder. He further stated that none is dedicated to Caesar or any of his followers and that almost exclusively all the participants in the dialogues are known enemies of Caesar, among them several who had been killed while fighting against him. Moreover, Strasburger stressed that Cicero in these late philosophical works, without mentioning names, often brands forms of conduct which must have reminded contemporary readers at once of Caesar.

There was, for instance, the dialogue *Hortensius* (now lost), set in one of the years between 62 and 60 B.C. The participants are Cicero, Hortensius, Catulus, and Lucullus. One is reminded that these were the four called upon first in the meetings of the Senate in 62 as being the most eminent *viri consulares* and that Hortensius had been the principal target of Cicero when, during and after his exile, he complained of the jealousy and the betrayal which he had experienced from the optimates. The *Hortensius* treatise, then, might be a belated apology to him and to those whom Cicero had maligned at that earlier time, and eventually deserted in April 56.

The same participants, Catulus, Hortensius, and Lucullus, reappear a little later in the *Academica priora*. The *Academica posteriora* is dedicated to Marcus Varro, also a participant in the dialogue, together with Cicero and Atticus. He had fought against Caesar in Spain. There is more: in *About the Ends of Goods and Evils* we find among the participants Marcus Cato, Lucius Manlius Torquatus, Gaius Valerius Triarius, and Marcus Pupius Piso. Cato, of course, was eulogized by Cicero above all else. Torquatus, a former praetor, had likewise committed suicide after the battle of Thapsus; Triarius had been killed by Caesar's army in the battle of Pharsalus; Piso had once been Cicero's companion in Greece and his son fought against Caesar in 49.[38] Publius Nigidius Figulus, a participant in Cicero's dialogue *Timaeus*, was also an eminent follower of Pompey.[39] He had already died in exile in 45 B.C. when Cicero wrote the treatise.

These facts clearly indicate that, by the summer of 45, Cicero had abandoned any hope or expectation he might have had concerning Caesar. By now, more than ever, he condemned Caesar and idealized his enemies. Early in May 45, Caesar's *Anticato* had become known. Caesar complimented Cicero on the style of his *Cato*, but was obviously extremely angered by its substance. Atticus expected trouble and at his suggestion, Cicero, to placate Caesar, began to write a "letter of advice" (*Symbouleutikon*) addressed to him in the style of the memoirs sent by Aristotle and Theopompus to Alexander the Great.[40] A few days later, the letter was shown to Caesar's intimates, Balbus and Oppius. As Cicero already suspected, they were not satisfied. They requested a number of changes which Cicero (who, it seems, had already gone farther than he had intended) was in no mood to make. He withdrew the pamphlet and told Atticus: "I am even afraid he might take it as intended for a kind of peace-offering after the *Cato*."[41] He was ashamed of having tried.[42] Although as late as July he toyed with the idea of addressing Caesar on the topic of the constitution,[43] he now despaired of accomplishing anything beyond (possibly) a higher degree of protection against potential harm from enemies who had influence with Caesar.

While personal relations between Cicero and Caesar, infrequent as they now had become, continued in civilized, if superficial fashion,[44] their discord had by now grown beyond remedy. Caesar acted in an increasingly autocratic fashion. He openly showed and publicly expressed his contempt for the commonwealth, calling the Republic a corpse and assuming for himself the place of the law.[45] The verdict was premature. Once he had accepted the permanent dictatorship early in February 44 B.C. (instead of the annual and renewable one), thus abandoning any pretense of temporary rule, some sixty people united in the name of the Republic to slay the tyrant. Caesar was assassinated in the Curia on 15 March 44, on the eve of his departure for war against the Parthians.

Although Cicero had no part in the plot, the fact that his friend Marcus Brutus was its driving force shows that he, too, must share the responsibility for it. For some time now, he had constantly reminded Brutus of what his ancestors had once accomplished. Not for nothing did Marcus Brutus, immediately after the assassination, shout Cicero's name and congratulate him on the revival of the Republic.[46] It was not without justification either that, in September, Marcus Antonius accused Cicero of having been the plot's spiritual instigator.[47] Cicero had become the symbol of the Republic, just as Caesar had become the token of monarchy and despotism. Cicero himself, years ago, had written in his *Republic* that it was every citizen's duty to fight against a tyrant for the freedom of his fellow-citizens.[48] He had long been familiar, at least since his first visit to Athens in 79 B.C., with the Athenian tyrannicides, Harmodius and Aristogiton. He knew that they received official cult as heroes, he had seen their statues. Athenian coins minted shortly before his arrival depicted them in the act of slaying the tyrant and must have gone through his hands. He had made much of the two heroes in his speech for Milo (whom he depicted as another tyrant-slayer).[49] While Cicero was certainly not the only one responsible for creating and spreading the ideology which led to Caesar's assassination, it would be a mistake to deny his share.

Not only did he approve of the deed, but he was jubilant, despite the fact that more than once he had experienced Caesar's generosity and favor. Distasteful as such jubilation is, it shows how deeply Caesar had hurt his vital feelings and that the personal kindness extended to himself did not compensate for the utmost contempt shown to the Republic and the constitution. Moreover, it was Caesar who had achieved what Cicero aspired to: "Far to excel, out-topping all the rest," and who had reduced him to a mediocre role.[50]

The conspirators—or liberators, as Cicero consistently called them—had expected that with the tyrant's removal, the Republic would automatically be restored. Instead, Caesar's fall created a political vacuum. Brutus and his followers showed less determination to fill it than Cicero thought necessary, and the initiative shifted to the adherents of Caesar. On their side, Marcus Antonius, the surviving consul, as holder of the highest office, was in a better position to act than the conspirators, among whom Brutus and Cassius as praetors were the highest ranking magistrates. The danger of immediate violence was averted when the Senate, convened by Antonius, settled for a compromise on 17 March. It was acknowledged that Caesar had been slain by patriotic citizens (Shakespeare's "honourable men") who were not to be prosecuted, but at the same time it was agreed that Caesar's *acta* would remain valid, including his appointments of magistrates and governors for several years in advance. The settlement prevented another Civil War since the formula was meant to do justice to both Caesar and his assassins. Nevertheless, it put the latter in a defensive position. That they were granted immunity implied that they had committed a crime, not performed a citizen's duty. This settlement was drawn up by the joint efforts of Antonius and Cicero, described in Cicero's language as follows: "I laid the foundations of peace" ("ieci fundamenta pacis").[51]

Tensions remained, however, and soon grew when Caesar's will, with its popular provisions, became known. From April on, Gaius Octavius, an eighteen-year-old youth, the son of Caesar's niece Atia, deliberately stirred things up. He appeared in Rome as Caesar's posthumously adopted son; as a consequence of the adoption, he changed his name to Gaius Iulius Octavianus (Octavian in short), and soon to Gaius Caesar. He went, however, far beyond posing as Caesar's son; he claimed to be his political heir and demanded revenge for his murder. He strongly appealed to many bound by loyalty or interest to Caesar's cause. Antonius, who initially seemed to be their natural leader, felt a strong challenge, but was restricted in his actions by the agreement of 17 March. Octavian created a dilemma for him, since Antonius was neither prepared to resign as the leader of Caesar's party, nor to break that agreement. He even earned praise from Cicero for his conduct in the first weeks after the Ides of March. These turbulent events, so well documented, need not be retold here; an authoritative account may be found in the appropriate chapters of Syme's *Roman Revolution*. By October 44, the situation had changed to the point that Brutus and Cassius left Italy in an attempt to gain a more solid footing in the eastern provinces, while the rivalry between Octavian and Antonius had come close to open war. Antonius was supposed to govern Macedonia in 43, but had this disposition overturned by a law which assigned to him Gallia Cisalpina instead. That province, the keystone to the military control of Italy, was presently governed by Decimus Brutus, one of Caesar's assassins. Since Antonius foresaw that Brutus might refuse to surrender the province to him, he had four legions come to Italy from Macedonia to strengthen his hand. This alarmed all those who sided with Caesar's murderers; it also alarmed Octavian who was afraid of being overwhelmed by force. He now illegally recruited an army in Campania from among Caesar's veterans and then, having secured control of the treasure which Caesar had sent ahead for the Parthian War, bribed two of the four legions of the consul to desert to him.

In another major development, Antonius and Cicero, the two men who had jointly forged the compromise of 17 March, clashed and became deadly enemies. Cicero was mainly to blame for the rupture that took place in September following earlier frictions. On the first day of that month, the Senate met to discuss some posthumous honors for Caesar. That was part of Antonius's strategy to regain some ground lost to Octavian within his own party. Cicero had excused himself under some pretext, with good reason: if present, he would have been among the first called upon and forced to speak about Caesar. Antonius criticized his absence before the house with a general attack on Cicero. Cicero could have ignored it, but this would not have been in character. He appeared the following day and replied more harshly than necessary (first Philippic). Matters now escalated; on 19 September, Antonius answered in a well-prepared speech in the Senate. Cicero, although absent, felt badly hurt (Antonius had touched some very sensitive spots) and lashed out at him with a vitriolic speech which, although never delivered, purported to be Cicero's immediate answer to the consul's attack. This is the second Philippic, where Antonius is depicted as Public Enemy Number One, a Catilina, Clodius, and Caesar all in one person. The speech was not published at the time, certainly not before Antonius's departure from the city late in November, perhaps not at all during Cicero's lifetime.

A uniquely brilliant pamphlet, it lacks a clear political direction. It rather looks as if a pre-existing antipathy on Cicero's part increased to uncontrolled anger when the consul attacked him as a provincial upstart and a political turncoat. If that is correct, then the explanation for this pamphlet belongs to the sphere of psychology. While Cicero almost identifies with the Republic[52] in the very first sentence, Antonius becomes the incarnation of all evil. Cicero had tied himself to the Republic before; already when he returned from exile in September 57, he had said that the Republic had been absent with him.[53] With Cato and so many others now dead, he had, in fact, become the symbol of the Republic, as Marcus Brutus demonstrated during the Ides of March.

Brutus, however, strongly differed with Cicero's assessment of the political situation, then and still much later. He always held that an understanding with Antonius was possible; and Antonius, for his part, as late as February 43 B.C., claimed that he was prepared to sign another agreement with Caesar's assassins.[54] Brutus clearly recognized that Octavian represented the real danger, "this very boy, who is apparently incited by Caesar's name against Caesar's killers."[55] He was right, as events were to show. Brutus, unfortunately, was no longer on the scene. Cicero, for his part, obsessed by his hate for Antonius, for that very reason thought him also the archenemy of republican government and liberty. He had to be defeated at all costs, even if to that end one had to temporarily associate with the devil.

Once again it fell to Cicero to come to the rescue of his country. As soon as Antonius left Rome on 28 November 44 B.C. to take over his province, Gallia Cisalpina, Cicero returned from the countryside to the city. "Adsum igitur," "I am present," he wrote on 6 December; "with these words Cicero closed this last letter to Atticus as if answering to his name as the Senate-roll was called."[56] Only a few months ago, he had tried to leave Italy, supposedly to visit his son in Athens, but really because of the seemingly desperate political situation. He had actually boarded the ship and sailed away, but a storm forced him to return. Cicero was soon grateful for it, since, had he left, he would have been viewed as a deserter. The storm, of course, had been no accident; the country itself had recalled him with its distinct voice, since it needed him in this hour of distress: "nisi me e medio cursu clara voce patria revocasset."[57] In such a mood, he had taken on Antonius in September.

Now, it was early December and Antonius had left. This time, Cicero, who in better causes had often vacillated, had often been faint-hearted, did not hesitate, did not shun any danger. He grabbed the helm with great determination and forced the ship to follow the course he directed. What he had to offer was the army of Octavian. For weeks, the young man had bombarded Cicero with messages to come to his aid and lend him his services. He had raised an army that might enable him to withstand Antonius. It was an illegal act, for which he desperately needed some belated authorization.[58] This could only come from the Senate and the man to manage it was Cicero. The bargain looked simple: Cicero was to obtain legality for Octavian and his army, in exchange for which Octavian would place himself and his army at the Senate's disposal. For the moment, that meant an alliance with Caesar's murderer, Decimus Brutus, who was not inclined to turn over his province to Antonius. Octavian, hostile as he was to all of Caesar's assassins, nevertheless accepted the alliance and postponed his revenge.

When the Senate met on 20 December, Cicero succeeded in obtaining approval of Octavian's actions and of Decimus Brutus's resistance against the consul Antonius. Moreover, the dispositions which the Senate had made three weeks earlier, at Antonius's motion, about the future governors of the provinces, were rescinded.[59] Most of these acts were against the law (a law had given Antonius Gallia Cisalpina and no decree of the Senate could ever invalidate a law). With all these motions (and others to follow soon), Cicero violated the constitution and abandoned the principles of republican government which he himself had taught and for which, he insisted, he was fighting right now.[60] He, of course, was fully aware of what he was doing and, therefore, mustered all his dialectical skills to create a smoke screen. This was no time for petty scruples; the country was in great danger and it had fallen to him and Octavian to rescue it. What they did was in the state's best interest, was intended to preserve the liberty of Rome that Antonius threatened and to restore the Republic. A legalist such as Marcus Cato would have been shocked, had he seen what was done in the name of lawful government. Anyhow, Cicero this time seemed to have what Cato hardly ever achieved—success.

In the end, though, his success benefited not the Republic, but Octavian. When, some fifty years later, the old emperor Augustus, who had once been Octavian, described his revolutionary beginnings, he used some euphemisms: "At the age of nineteen I raised an army on my own counsel and with private means; with it, I restored freedom for the state that had been oppressed by the tyranny of a clique."[61] These euphemistic expressions were exactly the same catchwords that Cicero had formulated at the time: "A young man . . . Gaius Caesar . . . raised a very strong army . . . and lavished his patrimony . . . From that scourge Caesar by his private initiative . . . delivered the Commonwealth."[62] The same events are very differently (and more correctly) described by Tacitus in a scene where the people attending the funeral of Augustus discuss his beginnings: "it was from the lust of dominion that he excited the veterans by his bounties, levied an army while yet a stripling and a subject, seduced the legions of a consul. . . ."[63]

For the moment, Cicero was not concerned that he had violated the constitution in order to rescue the Republic. Once Antonius was defeated, one would return to the rule of law and business as usual. He seems to have labored under the illusion that after the victory, the constitution would regain all its vital functions. It did not occur to him that the Republic might already be dead if it needed such remedies. To gain victory, the boy Octavian was indispensable; after the victory would come the right moment to clip his wings. Octavian, so Cicero said in private, "must get praises, honours, and—the push," "laudandum, ornandum, tollendum," where the last word may mean "exaltation," but is more naturally understood as "removal."[64] Cicero was not playing fair (he was, of course, shocked when he learned that his bon mot had been reported to Octavian). In the end, it was Octavian who double-crossed Cicero.

For the time being, things looked promising enough. On 20 December 44 B.C., Cicero once more became what he had been twenty years earlier, the politician of the hour. That day, in the absence of both consuls, Antonius and Dolabella, the tribunes had convened the Senate. The agenda was restricted to a single item: how to ascertain that the meeting scheduled for 1 January would be free from possible interference. The new consuls, Aulus Hirtius and Vibius Pansa, were to assume their duties at that meeting. Since a message from Decimus Brutus had just been received that he would not turn over Gallia Cisalpina to Antonius and was awaiting further orders from the Senate, Cicero jumped at the opportunity. He widened the debate into "a comprehensive survey of the political situation."[65] The result was approval of Brutus's resistance and legalization of Octavian's army. The Republic, so Cicero calculated, would have in him and Brutus two military leaders capable of crushing the new tyrant Antonius.

It is easy in hindsight to say that the Republic (and Cicero, for that matter) might have been better served, had Antonius been supported instead of Octavian. Marcus Brutus, for one, or Atticus,[66] did not need hindsight to see matters that way. Cicero, however, no longer had any choice after his break with Antonius. Had he avoided that rupture, he might have been able to side with Antonius against Octavian. But it remains doubtful whether he and the Republic would have fared any better in that case. And Cicero could not be expected to desert Decimus Brutus when he was attacked by Antonius. Not that he ever fully trusted Octavian; he was aware of the risk of concluding an alliance with him. But Antonius, too, while not quite the bête noire of the "Philippics," presented a real danger to the Republic. Moreover, the reverence shown to Cicero by Octavian made the recipient believe that he would be able to guide the young man, just as in 60 B.C. he had flattered himself that he would be able to guide Pompey and improve Caesar. Octavian with his army was a godsend, next to Cicero the savior and now the shield of the Republic. He was inspired by a god: what "if some higher power had not inspired Caesar Octavian?," Cicero asked Marcus Brutus in a letter.[67] True, he acted "of his own volition . . . though not without approbation and encouragement from me."[68] There was just one question: "what God then presented to us and to the Roman People this godlike young man?"[69]

The agreement reached in the Senate two days after Caesar's murder and which had prevented the outbreak of civil war was described by Cicero as follows: "I laid the foundations of peace." He commented in a similar way on his activity in the Senate on 20 December 44 B.C.: "I laid the foundations of the Commonwealth."[70] His initiative and leadership had once more ignited in the people the hope for liberty, so he said: "I led the recovery of freedom."[71] And he could add: "today . . . after a long interval, with me to prompt and to lead, our hearts have kindled to the hope of liberty."[72]

For seven eventful months, from December 44 to July 43 B.C., Cicero was in fact what he had always wanted to be, the leader of the state. He had no legal claim to such function, since he held no office, but he had a plan, he was determined—and he possessed authority. He was by now well over sixty, but he seemed rejuvenated, his energy was boundless, his enthusiasm inspiring. His message was simple: Antonius is the despot, the public enemy; he must be defeated; with him there can be no accommodation. Other leaders opposed such a rigid course and hesitated, but all those who tried to slow Cicero down were soon overrun by his drive and persistence. It was primarily Cicero who recruited the two consuls, Hirtius and Pansa, to the cause. Both were protégés of Caesar (Hirtius, in fact, is the author of the last book of Caesar's *Gallic War*); both had been Cicero's students in the art of oratory, and both were rivals of Antonius. At best, what could be expected from them was neutrality. Cicero nevertheless succeeded in making them obey the Senate as he made the Senate follow the course which he directed.[73] Public opinion, too, was important; Cicero, without fail, regularly addressed the people to explain and defend his policy; two of his "Philippic" speeches were not delivered in the Senate, but addressed directly to the people of Rome. Moreover, he was in touch with most provincial governors, working on each of them through letters and messages carefully phrased to influence the individual recipient.

During the winter, while Antonius was besieging Decimus Brutus in Mutina, Cicero made every effort to have Brutus relieved. The army of Octavian, consisting of the two veteran legions that had deserted Antonius and of Caesar's veterans recruited in Campania, was available. A second army now came into being, raised at the order of the Senate by the new consuls. Antonius realized that his position was deteriorating; he offered to negotiate and was prepared for major concessions, but Cicero managed to spoil the move. He did not want a peaceful settlement; he wanted Antonius defeated and destroyed. In that, he was as determined as he had been in the affair of Catilina and his followers. Cicero, in these months, presents the image of a man who had stored, during the previous twenty years, a large reserve of unused energies now bursting into action.

He came close to reaching his goal. At first, the forces of the Republic won big in the East. In February 43, Marcus Brutus reported that he had occupied Macedonia and Illyricum and contracted a large army. A little later came the news that Antonius's brother Gaius, the rightful governor of Macedonia, had been taken prisoner. Soon it was learned that Cassius had fared even better in Syria and Egypt and was now in command of a large number of legions. And now, there was also victory in Italy. At the end of April, in two engagements, the combined forces of the consuls and Octavian defeated Antonius near Mutina. With his army, Decimus Brutus was relieved and expected to go in hot pursuit of the enemy. When the news arrived in Rome, Cicero finally had the satisfaction of having Antonius outlawed. The Senate, for a long time unwilling to comply, despite Cicero's repeated and urgent demands, now declared him a public enemy, *hostis*. His collapse would only be a matter of days, so it seemed. The Republic was preserved and, after such victory, would be stronger than it had been for a very long time. All that was unquestionably Cicero's own doing. Once again, he had saved the country, neither as consul nor as general, this time, but as citizen and leading senator, a *princeps*. Once more, he received large ovations from the crowd.

Within a few weeks, everything was wrecked. Both consuls had been lost in battle (Pansa died of his wounds a few days later). This was an unforeseen calamity and delivered a most severe blow to Cicero's strategy. Moreover, Antonius had managed to escape across the Alps and to join three legions which one of his lieutenants succeeded in leading to him. He then won over the armies of two governors in Gaul and Spain, on whose loyalty Cicero had counted. They were Aemilius Lepidus and Munatius Plancus, both slick opportunists, in command of armies that now became Antonius's. To make matters worse, immediately after the victory, Octavian showed signs of hostility to Decimus Brutus, once a protégé of Caesar, who had joined the ranks of the assassins. Brutus was the first with whom the nemesis caught up. He soon found himself isolated, his troops deserted him, and while trying to make his way through the Alps to Marcus Brutus in Macedonia, he was betrayed and slain. Cicero now pinned his hope on Marcus Brutus and his army. Repeatedly, in more and more urgent terms, he called him back to Italy. Brutus, however, with or without good reason, was not prepared to listen.

Octavian now demanded the vacant consulship for himself (at nineteen, he was not even eligible for the minor offices) and suggested that Cicero be his colleague. When the Senate refused, he marched with his army upon Rome. He occupied the city in July and, after irregular elections, entered the consulship on 19 Sextilis 43 B.C., together with his relative Q. Pedius. This event, among others, later caused this month to be renamed "August."[74] Octavian prompted Pedius, a nephew or grandnephew of Caesar, to introduce a bill which outlawed Caesar's murderers (*Lex Pedia*) and another which rehabilitated Antonius and Lepidus (the Senate had declared Lepidus an enemy once he had joined Antonius). Octavian then left Rome to meet them near Bologna. The three concluded a pact (the second triumvirate) in November, as a result of which they grabbed all power in the state for five years. Following Sulla's example, they drew up a list of enemies to be outlawed and stripped of their fortunes. Among the first to be killed was Cicero, on 7 December 43 B.C.[75]

Several months earlier, in his last preserved letter to Marcus Brutus, dated 27 July, he had expressed, for the first time, uneasiness about Octavian: "As I write I am in great distress because it hardly looks as though I can make good on my promises in respect of the young man, boy almost, for whom I went bail to the commonwealth."[76] He always knew that entering into an alliance with Caesar's heir was a very risky business, but even if he had underestimated the extent of that risk, he no longer had a choice, when the opportunity of such an alliance presented itself. After Octavian occupied Rome in July and all senators came to pay their respects, Cicero, too, eventually appeared. He was greeted with the words: "Look here, the last of my friends." He requested, and received, exemption from the obligation to attend the Senate. He acknowledged this with two lines: "I am doubly pleased that you granted the exemption, since in doing this you pardon things past and allow for others to come."[77] There was, however, not to be any future for Cicero the politician. From the last four months of his life, there exists neither a single piece of information about him (except for his final day) nor a single word said or written by him.

Chapter Six

Epilogue

Cicero's last struggle for the Republic, the only one which had been entirely his, ended in failure. He paid with his life. The fact, however, that he faced the struggle, that he did not shy away from it and that he put into it all he had to give, does him honor. Under Caesar's rule he had often comforted himself with a maxim of the Stoics that a man's true value was not in what he accomplished, but in what he had striven after.[1]

This essay has followed Cicero's political career to the end, recording its ups and downs, a few sparkling highlights and large periods of impotence. A more general assessment of Cicero the politician is now in order. The usual verdict is that he was a failure, even if he had his moments, as when he crushed the Catilinarians in 63, when he withstood Caesar's offers, or when he mobilized the country against Antonius. This is not generally considered a great achievement for a political career which spanned over twenty years, even counting only from the consulship. In fairness to Cicero, however, it must be stressed that, except for the first three of these twenty years, conditions always prevailed which made it impossible for any Roman who was not one of the three men in power to pursue a constructive political career. Throughout the fifties, matters were firmly in the hands of the triumvirs. The attempt to break up their union when it appeared shaky, in the spring of 56, failed. When the alliance between Pompey and Caesar finally began to crumble, Cicero, as governor of Cilicia, was far removed from the scene of action. When he returned, war was already inevitable and was followed by Caesar's autocratic rule.

In all these years, from his own consulship in 59 to his murder in 44, Julius Caesar constituted the main obstacle not only for Cicero, but for any ambitious politician. His political talent, without any question, was far superior to that of any of his contemporaries. So was his instinct for, and his unscrupulous use of, power. What better proof is there of his political ability than that for many years he managed to keep things under control from far away, while he was conquering Gaul? The very years that were for Cicero years of inactivity and frustration, were for Caesar a time of continuous success. To avoid any personal setback, Caesar eventually went to war and, for more than four years, piled victory upon victory. In 44 B.C., he was the sole ruler of the Roman Empire, which he himself had considerably enlarged.

Those circumstances prevented Cicero from playing in politics the role that he might have played, had there not been such a dominant figure as Caesar. If Cicero, as a *homo novus,* was somewhat more open and more flexible in his political views than others, nevertheless there were boundaries which he hardly ever overstepped; whenever he did, he did not go far and it was not for long. Political convictions and a sense of propriety kept him within bounds. Those in power spared no effort to win his support because he was so talented, distinguished, and ambitious. Cicero could be seduced (or intimidated) to be more obliging than he wanted to be. But this is, by comparison, less surprising than the fact that whenever he had become entangled, he sooner or later extricated himself. Moreover, he always remained loyal to his basic convictions, resisting temptation and, occasionally, danger. His political credo, somewhat simplified, can be described as republican and conservative, but free of dogmatism.[2] He despised both monarchic and democratic rule; it was for the aristocracy to govern, as personified in the Senate and, above all, in the *viri consu-*

lares. Nevertheless, the superior magistrates, as relics of the old monarchy, and the people and their advocates, the tribunes, had certain constitutional rights which Cicero did not want to see either abolished or at the mercy of noble cliques.

Cicero never departed from these views.[3] As a politician and patriot, his conscience often denied him the opportunity of seeking advantage in ways that were routine for other politicians such as Caesar. Cicero had none of the unscrupulous manner that characterized, for instance, two of the brightest youths in the ranks of the oligarchs, Gaius Scribonius Curio and Marcus Caelius Rufus. For a long time, Cicero had been a paternal friend to both, but eventually they defected to Caesar for opportunistic reasons. Their treachery deeply hurt their former mentor.[4]

Cicero, it is true, was sometimes too obliging or too timid. He collapsed in the spring of 56 B.C. just when he was about to initiate an attack on Caesar: the violent reaction so intimidated him that he even began to serve Caesar's interests and those of Caesar's partners. In 49, he was so reluctant to abandon the hope that he might be able to negotiate peace, that he arrived too late at the camp to which he belonged, when people had almost given up waiting for him. After the battle of Pharsalus, he felt that the cause was lost, while others continued fighting. Although hardly to blame for his judgment, he must be blamed for his rash decision to return to Italy, instead of retreating to a quiet place in the Greek world, outside Caesar's immediate realm. All these shortcomings are only too well known, mostly through his own testimony.

However, there is also the other side of the coin: the man who, whenever he fails in such a way, first always blames others (the optimates, Pompey, etc.), but soon, tortured by his conscience, admits that he has behaved wrongly, or dishonorably. Cicero acknowledged that his speech *On the consular provinces* in June 56 was a disgraceful piece. In 49, he first wanted to make Pompey and himself believe that he could not have left Italy with Pompey's army because Caesar had already cut him off. But he soon confessed that he had not really tried: "Still, I may as well acknowledge what is the fact—I did not try very hard," and later that he had been too timid: "I stayed in Italy as long as I was able. But sensibility prevailed with me over fear. I was ashamed to fail Pompey in his hour of need."[5]

Time and again, Cicero pulled himself together; humiliation and ignominy then forced him to do what was right, not what was profitable, to choose the *honestum,* not the *utile.* Against his better interest, he defended Milo in 52, he resisted Caesar's offers,[6] he withstood the pressure to pose as a mediator from Rome, that is to say, from Caesar's camp. He also left Italy for Pompey's headquarters at a time when Caesar was winning and Pompey was losing, despite explicit warnings from Caesar and his own fear. He openly told Caesar that it had been on his impulse, not his brother's, that the two had joined the enemy.[7] He praised Cato, glorifying the man who had always accused Caesar of despotism, and he sent his pamphlet to Caesar. He intimated in the dictator's presence that Caesar's cause in the Civil War had been inferior to that of the losing side.[8] He spoke before the dictator with great frankness in favor of those who were not yet pardoned and about the state that needed rebuilding. He told Caesar that all his victories would be for nothing if he were not to restore the Republic.[9] His friends began to fear that Cicero might get hurt by such candor; they persuaded him to write something obliging and send it to Caesar. Cicero tried, but then destroyed the draft when he realized that Caesar would not welcome what he could honestly say and that he could not honestly say anything that might please Caesar.

Over a span of fifteen years, from Caesar's consulship in 59 to his assassination in 44 B.C. and beyond, Cicero, in commenting on the affairs of the commonwealth, time and again expressed feelings of impotence: first toward the three rulers, and then when he realized that nothing could prevent the Civil War. This feeling also accounted for his expectation that everything would be at the mercy of the victor (whoever he might be). Caesar's omnipotence confirmed the feeling and Antonius's conduct after Caesar's assassination rekindled it. Whenever Cicero deplored his own impotence regarding those in power, he also deplored that of the other *boni* and that of the Republic. Despite his ambition and conceit, he was not entirely self-centered. He did not lament only the loss of personal power and influence, but also the fact that a single man had arrogated powers that used to be divided among a multitude. In *De re publica,* he had described the Roman constitution as a perfect mixture of the three model constitutions: monarchy, aristocracy, and democracy. The Republic meant much more to him than just a beautiful image and it does not matter to what extent his description of it resembled the realities of his day. Rome had become the ruler of the world, thanks to the supremacy of its constitution. Obvious deviations from it were not the result of changing conditions within the Roman world, but of the activity of scoundrels, *improbi.* What was needed were not constitutional changes, but a new morality. Cicero was as incapable as most of his contemporaries of identifying the objective conditions that caused the crisis of the state—for instance, the difficulty, or impossibility, of governing the world through institutions created for a city community.[10] In his view, real problems became personal and were categorized as right or wrong, good or evil. As Hegel saw:[11] "Cicero . . . always attributes the corrupt state of the republic to individuals and their passions." The battle was between the *boni* and the *improbi,* between those who wanted to preserve an order that had worked well in the days of Scipio Aemilianus and Laelius the Sage and those who put their own personal interests before those of the commonwealth.

Among the latter he placed not only Caesar and Antonius, but Pompey also. He and Caesar were competing for monarchic rule and from the victor, whoever he might be, Cicero only expected what Rome had experienced before: proscriptions and confiscations. He called Pompey a "king," just like Caesar; but there is one difference: "This is a fight for a throne. The expelled monarch is the more moderate, upright, and clean-handed, and unless he wins, the name of the Roman people must inevitably be blotted out; but if he does win, his victory will be after the Sullan fashion and example."[12]

After Pompey's death, the only king left was Caesar. For several years, Cicero was torn between the notion that the Republic was lost forever and the hope that it might still be revived by Caesar as it had once been revived by Sulla. He never left the slightest doubt that he abhorred any kind of government where one man rules alone, be it called *regnum, tyrannis,* or *dominatio* (that did not matter at all). If magistrates were appointed by one man instead of being elected by the people; if the Senate were only permitted to decree what the ruler wanted done; if a single man assumed the functions of the jury and administered justice instead of the people—then there could be no *res publica,* no commonwealth. Cicero has always been consistent in condemning these deviations from the constitution. He stated more than once that life under a monarch was not worth living.[13] As soon as he lost any illusion that Caesar might abdicate and reinstate some form of republican government, he turned irrevocably and violently against him.

Caesar's personality and career have always cast a spell on people's imagination, nowhere more so than in Germany. This has much to do with the country's history and its circumstances in the early nineteenth century. It was the time following the Napoleonic oppression, the time when Germany longed (as did Italy) to be at last united in a single state and, to that end, was looking for a strong man who might bring about political unity. The philosopher Georg Friedrich Hegel, while acknowledging that Caesar strove after personal goals, laid the basis for his glorification when he stated that they were identical with what was objectively needed. In his 1831 lectures on the philosophy of history, Hegel called Caesar one of those great men in history whose individual goals comprise the substance of what a higher order of the world demands.[14] He continues: "In this way the world-wide sovereignty of Rome became the property of a single possessor. This important change must not be regarded as a thing of chance; it was *necessary*—postulated by the circumstances. The democratic constitution could no longer be really maintained."[15]

Hegel deeply influenced Mommsen[16] with these views and, directly or through Mommsen, innumerable other scholars. The Republic was doomed, monarchy an absolute necessity; Caesar did what was called for, whether aware of it or (as Hegel wanted to have it) as an agent or instrument of a higher power ("Geschäftsführer des Weltgeistes"), only partially conscious of what he was doing. Long after Mommsen, the glorification of Caesar received another push with a famous book by a literary critic, a member of the circle of the poet Stefan George, Friedrich Gundolf. In 1925, he published his *Caesar: Geschichte seines Ruhmes* (Caesar: History of his Renown) and in 1926 a second book on Caesar in the nineteenth century. For Gundolf, Caesar was the greatest hero in all history. Gundolf accepts as reliable evidence only what Caesar himself has written.[17] He admired the fact that Caesar was equally brilliant in political and military actions and as a writer.[18] And the personality that comes across in Caesar's writings is indeed tremendously appealing, as long as one is prepared to accept the author's word and to be lulled by his bewitching charm.[19] Gundolf wrote shortly after Germany's defeat in World War One and after the inglorious end of the German and Austrian monarchies, at the time when there was once more a widespread longing for a strong man, this time not to unite, but to resurrect the nation. The opening sentence of his earlier book on Caesar sets the note: "Today, as the need for a strong man is articulated . . . we wish to remind the overeager of the *great man* . . . Caesar."

This admiration for Caesar always makes Cicero look bad in comparison. Works of the most learned, intelligent, and honest scholars, like Matthias Gelzer, who wrote monographs on both, demonstrate this fact.[20] The question, however, is whether such admiration for Caesar the politician or the statesman is justified (as distinct from Caesar the general, the writer, the charismatic human being). This has sometimes been denied—for instance, a few years before Hegel, by such a perceptive mind as Barthold Georg Niebuhr. He thought it worthy of note that nowhere in all that Caesar did is there any inkling that he ever thought of reforming the constitution and ending the anarchy. Niebuhr goes on to say that all of Caesar's reforms were, in fact, unessential, and that, unlike Sulla, he apparently had no idea of how to solve the constitutional problem.[21] However, the view of Hegel and of Mommsen prevailed. In the recent past, the late Hermann Strasburger effectively questioned the notion of Caesar, the great statesman, in a long paper, "Caesar im Urteil seiner Zeitgenossen" (Caesar as judged by his contemporaries).[22]

Strasburger's thesis is that Caesar knew how to acquire monarchical power, but did not know what to do with it. Strasburger presents the evidence of all witnesses and demonstrates that, without exception, they condemned the fact that Caesar resorted to force against his country. Many of those were his adherents and had personal or political ties with him, or both. Even those closest to Caesar were convinced that he had no intention of restoring anything like a republican constitution and no concept at all for the reorganization of the state.[23] Strasburger's teacher, Matthias Gelzer, whose monograph on Caesar bears the subtitle "Politician and Statesman," had attributed to Caesar qualities of statesmanship which Strasburger questioned. Gelzer, at the urgent request of German schoolteachers, then reacted with the essay "Was Caesar a Statesman?" in which he defended his opinion.[24] Strasburger replied in a postscript to a second edition of his paper.[25] Gelzer's main point was that an individual who brings about as much change as Caesar did, and who thereby determines the direction of future developments, deserves the epithet of statesman.[26] He did not really address the issue of whether Caesar's political activity was as creative, or as beneficial, as it was destructive. For his part, Strasburger conceded, some twenty years after he wrote the original manuscript, that he would be less dogmatic in his judgment of Caesar as being no statesman, but he stood firm by his main conclusions.[27]

If these are correct, as it seemed to others and now to me,[28] this adds an additional burden on Caesar's decision to cross the Rubicon[29] and at the same time argues for a more positive appreciation of those who slew him. They have generally been charged with the fact that after Caesar's assassination, civil war raged for another fourteen years over large parts of the empire in west and east. Accordingly, Caesar's assassination has been called a senseless deed, a crime, and a mistake.[30] It is true, some of the conspirators had personal grievances against Caesar, others had prospered thanks to him, and others had reasons to be both grateful to and angry with him. All that does not matter in the least, as long as it cannot be excluded that Caesar was murdered for what he had done to the state, the constitution, and a tradition sanctified by centuries. He had overturned it all for personal goals,[31] fully aware of what he was doing, since he was quoted as saying that crossing the Rubicon would bring misfortune to mankind, while renunciation would spell trouble for himself.[32] Such presumption cannot be justified unless in due course it leads to improved conditions of life for a substantial part of those ruled. Caesar did not show even the least inclination of bringing about anything of the kind—at the time of his murder, he was not trying to heal the wounds of the Civil War, but was on the eve of a war against the Parthians.[33]

The fact that the Civil War continued after his assassination was as much a consequence of his crossing the Rubicon and his decision to cling to monarchical power as it was a consequence of his murder. Several indications suggest that, in the end, both Cicero and Brutus might have forgiven him for having waged war on the Republic; they could not, however, forgive the man who, in action and in words, pronounced the Republic dead. His assassination was a crime, no doubt, but it was also a moral event.[34] It is impossible to know whether Caesar's rule or that of the sons of Pisistratus of Athens weighed heavier on their respective subjects, and this, in fact, does not matter much. What matters is that their subjects used to be free, and that some among them were determined to regain that freedom, by violent action, if that was the only way. While grateful Athenian citizens celebrated and worshipped the Athenian tyrant-slayers as heroes, Brutus and Cassius, whose statues the Athenians in 44 put next to those of their own heroes,[35] soon became nonpersons in Rome: to mention them honorably was a crime; their portraits were not allowed to be carried among twenty others in the funeral procession for Cassius's widow, Brutus's sister Iunia, sixty-three years after their deaths.[36]

The difference in appreciation is, of course, due to the fact that in Athens freedom (and democracy) eventually resulted from the violent deed, while in Rome monarchy obtained the upper hand. One may say (with Hegel) that this result was a *Necessity*,[37] but even if true, it would not be sufficient cause to condemn Caesar's assassins—whom Hegel himself called "the noblest men of Rome," singling out by name Cicero, Brutus, and Cassius.[38] If all of this leads to the conclusion that conventional judgment on Caesar and on his assassins must change, then it must of necessity change on Cicero, too.[39]

In this context, a word may be said about one of the most common objections raised against Cicero the politician, the charge that he was too often unsuccessful, *sans fortune,* and that he failed in his last (and most important) fight. Cicero himself felt that success in politics often passed him by. This made him stress his conviction that what a man had aimed at mattered more than what he had accomplished. More specifically, he said at least once in public, and in Pompey's presence, that he valued the inefficient resistance of the consul Bibulus against his colleague Caesar higher than all the victories and triumphs of the triumvirs.[40] Much as Cicero would have given to be a more successful politician than he was, he was not prepared to give all it might take to obtain success.[41] Wherever the question of success enters into a discussion of Cicero the politician, the contrasting figure is, of course, always Caesar, so strikingly the darling of *Fortuna.* Nevertheless, the comparison breaks down if one makes the measure of success not just the individual's goal (Caesar undoubtedly reached his, while Cicero failed), but the common good. Of the two, Caesar failed much more acutely in that respect, since he mainly achieved destruction, whereas Cicero fought for preservation. It may legitimately be questioned whether or not the state of affairs which Cicero tried to defend was worth preserving, but it is far from obvious that its destruction was beneficial or (as Hegel put it) necessary. If the Principate was, in fact, an improvement over the late Republic, Caesar should not be credited with Augustus's accomplishment. It has often been observed, and correctly so, that Cicero had no real sense of the serious social problems of his age.[42] However, none of his contemporaries actually possessed, or articulated, such an understanding, certainly not Caesar.[43] While there are certainly many reasons to find fault with Cicero, there is, despite Mommsen's opposite verdict, no valid reason to condemn Cicero as a poor politician while extolling Caesar as a creative statesman.

At about the time Cato took his own life, in the spring of 46 B.C., Cicero lamented, at the end of his *Brutus,* that he was born so late that he lived to see night falling over the state.[44] He wished he had been born a century earlier and had lived in the age of Scipio

Aemilianus, which in his imagination looked ideal. If he had, he would have lived a sheltered existence, but conditions would hardly have allowed him to find his vocation and to develop his rich talents to the fullest. In the middle of the second century B.C., Cicero would not have found circumstances that enabled him, a mere knight from Arpinum, to make his way into the leaders' circle and become the champion of Latin intellectuality that he did become in his own time. It has been said of him "he was born too late"[45] and that as "a born middle-of-the-roader" he was "unlucky enough to live in a period of extremism,"[46] but it seems obvious that it was precisely the conditions of the time that brought out the best in him and made him what he was. They often made him suffer, but they also allowed him to flourish.

It was during the last year of his life, when the dominant figure of Caesar was removed from the scene and the political situation was full of extremes, that Cicero the politician finally came into his own. His fight, as much a personal fight against Antonius as a principled struggle for the Republic, is generally appreciated as his best performance in politics, despite his eventual defeat.[47] It has already been observed that in the course of the struggle Cicero abandoned many legalistic principles, that he denied the consul Antonius his lawful position,[48] proposed illegal commissions for Decimus Brutus and Octavian, moved that Marcus Brutus and Gaius Cassius be entrusted with the provinces and armies of the lawful governors and commanders. It was special pleading all the way, ostensibly for the single purpose of preserving the Republic. It was Cicero who coined phrases such as "wherever in the world Cassius and Brutus are . . . there is the Commonwealth,"[49] or "both Brutus and Cassius have already been their own Senate on a number of occasions."[50] As for Cassius who occupied Syria and defeated the duly appointed governor Dolabella, Cicero appeals to an even higher authority to justify Cassius's conduct: "did not Gaius Cassius . . . set out from Italy with the design of keeping Dolabella out of Syria? Under what law, by what right? By the right which Jupiter himself established, that all things beneficial to the Commonwealth be held lawful and proper."[51] Cicero also argued that all the military forces belonged to the state (or, to the Senate and the Roman people), and therefore those who used them to attack the state lost by that very fact all their rights.[52]

Cicero certainly did not hesitate to abandon lawful procedure and legal principles in order to obtain what he viewed as the higher-ranking value: the preservation of the Republic. For his conduct, extenuating circumstances are easy to find; the situation was extreme and required extreme measures; success or failure would, in the end, determine right and wrong. And Cicero had valid reasons to do what he did, since the republican government, as R. E. Smith observed, despite all its failings and shortcomings, "carried none the less within itself the seeds of freedom, as the Imperial system never did; the *libertas* that Cicero cherished and defended was a truer and finer thing than anything Tacitus could know."[53]

While Cicero's efforts to preserve the Republic failed in the end, his last fight may not have been entirely in vain. The fact that, for the first time in his career, he risked his life for the cause he judged right, and that he lost it in consequence, atones for former failures. Without his last stand he could hardly have become the standard bearer of republican ideology for centuries to come. Only sixteen years after Cicero's death, Augustus claimed, once he had defeated Antonius, to have restored the Republic or, at least, some kind of a free state.[54] The words sound as if Cicero had dictated them, or as if Augustus wished to say: "I have done what Cicero in vain expected from Caesar." What matters here is not so much whether the assurance was true (or to what degree it might have been true), but that the sentence was phrased in such a way. It was a rebuttal of Caesar who had pronounced the Republic dead. It was, in fact, a concession to republican ideology insofar as Augustus had at least *to pretend* that the new state of affairs was not the private matter of a monarch, but still (or again) a public affair, a *res publica*. It has been said, with intentional exaggeration: "It was Cicero's doing that Octavian on January 13, 27 B.C., released the *res publica* from his dominance and returned it to Senate and People."[55]

The question of whether Cicero's ideas had any substantial impact on the Augustan system has been widely discussed, with equivocal results: some scholars affirm it, some deny it, and some say that one cannot be sure.[56] It is doubtful that any actual feature of the principate (such as the figure of the *princeps*) can be traced back to Cicero, but it is clear that elements of republican tradition went into the ideological foundations of the principate, and that the republican spirit continued to live under the modified monarchy.[57] Among those responsible for such *Nachwirkung* (after effects), certainly Cicero has the first and the strongest claim. Since it was Cicero who enriched and transformed republican ideology,[58] it was his legacy, more than anything else, that made it virtually impossible for Augustus to follow in Caesar's footsteps. Cicero, therefore, was responsible for the concessions which the new monarchic system made to republican tradition. Cicero has laid the foundations of the survival of republican spirit in the history of mankind. Cato, too, had a similar effect on later generations; he personified the republican ideals through his actions and even more through his death; Cicero did so first through his words, but in the end also through his political engagement.

At the beginning of his confrontation with Antonius, he remarked that he had lived long enough either for years or for glory. This was almost a repetition of what Caesar had said two years earlier and what Cicero at the time had vigorously disputed, since Caesar had not yet restored any constitutional order.[59] Cicero perished when the Republic for which he lived was doomed to die. He had, after all, not been very far from the truth when he identified himself with her at the beginning of the second Philippic, just as he braced himself for his last fight. Alfred Heuss has said of him: "Cicero, who on account of his whole personality could almost have given his name to the entire age of the late Republic, was not the man to himself personify the idea of the Republic. He knew of, but was not, that idea."[60] Others may prefer to think that in the end Cicero had, in fact, become the idea of the Roman Republic.

Chronological Table

146   Destruction of Carthage by Scipio Aemilianus, of
      Corinth by Lucius Mummius.

133   Destruction of Numantia by Scipio Aemilianus.
      Tribunate, reforms, and death of Tiberius Gracchus.
      133–129, war against Aristonicus, Asia becomes a
      Roman province.

129   Death of Scipio Aemilianus.

123   Tribunate and reforms of Gaius Gracchus. *Lex
      Sempronia de capite civis.*

122   Second tribunate of Gaius Gracchus.

121   First use of *senatus consultum ultimum,* death of Gaius
      Gracchus.

116   Birth of Marcus Terentius Varro.

115   Cicero's grandfather commended by consul Marcus
      Aemilius Scaurus.

Based on the chronological table, *Cambridge Ancient History,* vol. 9.

114	Birth of Hortensius Hortalus.
112–106	War against king Jugurtha of Numidia.
109	Birth of Titus Pomponius Atticus.
107	Gaius Marius, consul I, supersedes Metellus in command against Jugurtha.
106	Birth of Marcus Tullius Cicero (January) and of Pompey (September). Capture of Jugurtha by Cornelius Sulla.
105	Two consular armies in Gaul destroyed by Cimbri and Teutoni at Arausio.
104	Marius, consul II, reorganizes Roman army.
102	Marius, consul IV, defeats Teutoni near Aquae Sextiae.
101	Marius, consul V, and Catulus defeat Cimbri at Vercellae.
100	Marius, consul VI, suppresses riots in Rome; death of praetor Servilius Glaucia and of tribune Appuleius Saturninus. Birth of Caesar (July).
95	Lucius Licinius Crassus and Quintus Mucius Scaevola pontifex consuls; noncitizens expelled from Rome.
94	Gaius Coelius Caldus, a *homo novus,* consul. 94 (?), Mucius Scaevola pontifex governor of Asia.
91–88	Social War; Cicero serves under consul Pompeius Strabo (89) and consul Cornelius Sulla (88). Citizenship granted to Italians; the Rubicon becomes Rome's border in the North.
88	King Mithridates VI Eupator overruns Asia Minor; massacre of Romans and Italians. Athens joins Mithridates; Philo of Larisa, head of the Academy, flees

to Rome. Bill of tribune Sulpicius Rufus gives command in Asia to Marius (in place of Sulla). Sulla occupies Rome, repeals laws of Sulpicius; death of Sulpicius.

87   Marius and consul Cornelius Cinna occupy Rome; massacre. Sulla in Greece.

86   Death of Marius, consul VII.

85   Sulla concludes peace with Mithridates.

84   Cinna, consul IV, killed by mutineers.

82   Civil War, victories of Sulla, death of the younger Marius. Proscriptions.

81   Sulla dictator; constitutional settlement; the Senate restored to power. Cicero's *pro Quinctio.*

80   Cicero's *pro Roscio Amerino.* Abdication of Sulla.

79–77   Cicero in Athens, Rhodes, and Asia Minor.

78   Death of Sulla. 78–77, attempt at overthrow of Sullan constitution by Aemilius Lepidus (consul 78) fails.

77   Cicero returns to Rome.

75   *Lex Aurelia* relieves tribunes of disability to hold other offices. Cicero quaestor in Western Sicily.

74–63   Third Mithridatic War; Lucius Licinius Lucullus given command against Mithridates.

73   Cicero member of the consul's *consilium* in the affair of the tax collectors versus the sanctuary of Amphiaraus.

70   First consulship of Pompey and Crassus. Restoration of full tribunician powers. Trial of Gaius Verres; Cicero's Verrine orations. *Lex Aurelia* changes composition of juries.

69   Cicero aedile. Lucullus invades Armenia, captures Tigranocerta.

67   *Lex Gabinia* gives Pompey command against pirates.

66   Cicero praetor, presides over the extortion court. *Lex Manilia* gives Pompey command against Mithridates; Cicero's *De lege Manilia.*

64   Quintus Cicero's *Commentariolum petitionis;* Cicero elected to the consulship.

63   Cicero consul; his speeches *De lege agraria; pro C. Rabirio.* Caesar elected pontifex maximus. Birth of Octavius (later Augustus). Conspiracy of Catilina; Cicero's *in Catilinam.* 5 December, execution of five Catilinarians. 10 December, tribune Metellus Nepos attacks Cicero. Death of Mithridates; Pompey organizes his conquests in the East.

62   1 January, Cicero *primus rogatus* in the Senate. Defeat and death of Catilina. Bona Dea scandal in Caesar's house. (December) Pompey lands in Italy and disbands his army. Cicero's *pro Sulla.*

61   The Senate opposes Pompey and Crassus. Publius Clodius acquitted of sacrilege.

60   First triumvirate.

59   Caesar consul. His bills in favor of Pompey and Crassus (tax farmers). *Lex Vatinia* gives Caesar Cisalpine Gaul and Illyricum for five years, the Senate adds Transalpine Gaul (Narbonensis). Cicero's defense of Gaius Antonius, Clodius adopted by a plebeian.

58   Lucius Calpurnius Piso and Aulus Gabinius consuls, Clodius tribune. *Lex Clodia de provinciis consularibus* gives Macedonia to Piso, Syria to Gabinius. Cato sent

to annex Cyprus. Cicero exiled. Caesar in Gaul, defeats Helvetii and Ariovistus.

57 4 September, Cicero returns to Rome. Pompey commissioner for grain supply.

56 Cicero attempts to destroy the triumvirate; his *in Vatinium*. (April) Conference at Luca. (May) Cicero's motions in favor of Caesar; his *De provinciis consularibus; pro Balbo*.

55 Elections delayed; Pompey and Crassus consuls II. *Lex Trebonia* gives Pompey Spain, Crassus Syria for five years each. *Lex Pompeia Licinia* extends Caesar's command in Gaul for another five years. Cicero defends Vatinius; his *De oratore*.

54 Rioting and scandals long prevent consular elections. Cicero's *pro Scauro*. (September) Death of Caesar's daughter Julia, wife of Pompey. Cicero testifies against Gabinius, then unsuccessfully defends him in another trial. Ps. Sallust, *In M. Tullium Ciceronem Invectiva*.

53 Continued rioting between the gangs of Clodius and Annius Milo. Defeat and death of Crassus near Carrhae in Mesopotamia. Cicero co-opted into the collegium of augurs.

52 (January) Murder of Clodius, followed by riots. Pompey sole consul (until August); he restores order, his laws. Trial of Milo, Cicero's *pro Milone*. Law of the ten tribunes grants Caesar permission to register his candidacy for another consulship *in absentia*. General revolt in Gallia under Vercingetorix, who finally surrenders at Alesia. Cicero successfully prosecutes Munatius Plancus Byrsa.

51 Consul Marcus Marcellus fails to have Caesar

recalled. Cicero's *De re publica.* Cicero governor of Cilicia.

50   Tribune Curio foils attempts to have Caesar recalled. Death of Hortensius. (November) Cicero returns to Rome, but stays in the suburbs, keeping his *imperium.*

49   (January) Caesar crosses the Rubicon, Civil War. 17 March, Pompey leaves Italy. 28 March, Caesar visits Cicero, who on 7 June follows Pompey to Greece. Caesar dictator, defeats Pompey's army in Spain.

48   9 August, Caesar defeats Pompey at Pharsalus; assassination of Pompey in Egypt; Caesar in Egypt, Alexandrian War. Cicero stranded at Brindisi.

47   Caesar in Egypt, Syria, and Asia; defeats Pharnaces of Bosporus, returns in September to Italy, pardons Cicero, and leaves for Africa.

46   6 April, Caesar defeats Metellus Scipio and King Juba at Thapsus; suicide of Cato at Utica. Four triumphs of Caesar; he pardons Marcus Marcellus; Cicero's *pro Marcello;* his *pro Ligario, Brutus.* Caesar leaves for Spain.

45   (March) Caesar defeats the sons of Pompey at Munda. Cicero's *Cato,* Caesar's *Anticato.* (Summer) Cicero calls Caesar "king."

44   (February) Caesar *dictator perpetuus.* 15 March, his assassination. Marcus Antonius surviving consul, Publius Dolabella *consul suffectus.* Appearance of Octavius, soon to be Gaius Caesar. Cicero's *De officiis, de divinatione.* (September) His falling-out with Antonius. His pact with Octavian. 20 December, Cicero obtains commissions for Octavian and Decimus Brutus in the Senate. He becomes the unofficial leader of the state.

43   Civil War *(bellum Mutinense)*. Cicero's *Philippics*.
       (April) Octavian and consuls Hirtius and Pansa defeat
       Antonius at Modena; death of both consuls. Antonius
       escapes across the Alps and gains armies in Gaul.
       (August) Octavian occupies Rome, elected consul;
       outlaws Caesar's assassins, rehabilitates Antonius.
       (November) Triumvirate with Antonius and Lepidus;
       proscriptions. 7 December, assassination of Cicero.

Notes

Chapter One. Cicero and the Late Republic

1. Crawford, *Orations*, 12. See, however, J. Korpanty, *Gnomon* 57 (1985), 750–51, who shows that the number of known speeches is even higher.
2. Other instances are *Orat.* 148; *Tusc.* 3.83; *Off.* 2.2: "Now, as long as the state was administered by the men to whose care she had voluntarily entrusted herself, I devoted all my effort and thought to her. But when everything passed under the absolute control of a despot and there was no longer any room for statesmanship or authority of mine . . . I did not resign myself to grief"; 3.1: "for as I am kept by force of armed treason away from practical politics and from my practice at the bar, I am now leading a life of leisure"; 3.3: "But my leisure is forced upon me by want of public business, not prompted by any desire for repose. For now that the senate has been abolished and the courts have been closed, what is there, in keeping my self-respect, that I can do either in the senate-chamber or in the forum?" See also 1.19; *Fam.* 9. 8.2 (letter to Varro).
3. Bringmann, *Untersuchungen,* 11. 183. 252–55. Stockton, *Cicero,* 270: "But for all his literary greatness, Cicero was essentially a political animal."
4. Zielinski, *Cicero im Wandel der Jahrhunderte;* Ferguson, "Some Ancient Judgments."
5. Drumann, *Geschichte Roms.* For Cicero, see 5.216–724; 6.1–685, esp. 419 ff. The work has been called "the most bizarre product of Ger-

man erudition" by Meyer, *Caesars Monarchie,* vi, and his verdict was judged to be "hard but not unjustified" by P. Groebe, who spent more than thirty years (1897–1929) bringing Drumann's work up to date (2nd ed., 6.viii). In Groebe's edition, the parts on Cicero are 5.230–708; 6.1–604, esp. 369 ff.

6. Th. Mommsen, *Römische Geschichte* 3 (1856); here quoted from the English edition, *The History of Rome,* trans. W. P. Dickson, vol. 4 (New York, 1894). Among other things, Cicero is labeled "notoriously a political trimmer" (208); "the mouthpiece of servility" (378); "As a statesman without insight, opinion, or purpose, he figured successively as democrat, as aristocrat, and as a tool of the monarchs, and was never more than a short-sighted egotist" (724).

7. Drumann-Groebe 6.viii.

8. See Bibliography for references to the works of these scholars, as well as for that of Thompson, referred to in the text.

9. See now, after many earlier expressions, Alföldi, *Caesar in 44 v. Chr.,* passim, esp. 367–86.

10. Syme, *Roman Revolution,* 137–39, 143–44, 146. See the sensible criticism of A. E. Douglas, *g & r,* new surveys 2 (1968), 4, 6–7, 10, and that of Bringmann, *Untersuchungen,* 349–50. See also Mitchell, *Cicero,* 106.

11. Meier, "Ciceros Consulat," 111.

12. This is why he said he would never have time to read poetry (he mentioned lyrics in particular), even if his life span were to be doubled (Sen. *ep.* 49.5: "Negat Cicero, si duplicetur sibi aetas, habiturum se tempus, quo legat lyricos").

13. "Nemo me minus timidus, nemo tamen cautior" (*Phil.* 12.24).

14. Cic. *Verr.* 2.4.147. The crime was that he addressed a council of subjects at all; that he did it in their Greek language was "intolerable by any means," "id ferri nullo modo posse."

15. Sen. *De brev. vit.* 5.1: "unable as he was to be restful in prosperity or patient in adversity." Seneca echoes here Asinius Pollio's words, quoted by his father (*Suas.* 6.24): "Would that he could have shown more temperateness in prosperity, more stoutness in adversity!" Ferguson, "Some Ancient Judgments," 19.

16. A. Heuss, *Römische Geschichte* (Braunschweig, 1960), 183. See also Klingner, "Cicero," 142: "A man such as Cicero will . . . always . . . be among those who suffer from history rather than among those who make it."

17. For a brief summary of the main data and sources, see Gelzer, *Cicero,* 1–28; for a full and sensible treatment of these earliest stages of Cicero's career, see Mitchell, *Cicero,* 1–92.

18. See A. Heuss, "Der Untergang der römischen Republik und das Problem der Revolution," *HZ* 182 (1956), 1–28; idem, *HZ* 216 (1973),

52–63, 71–72; J. F. McGlew, *Phoenix* 40 (1986), 424–45.

19. Meier, *Res publica amissa*, 201–5; in addition, from the 2nd edition (Berlin, 1980), xxi, xliii-liii. See, however, the critical remarks of A. Heuss, *HZ* 237 (1983), 87.

20. Gruen, *Last Generation*. His view has been criticized by P. Cartledge, *Hermathena* 119 (1975), 85–86; T. J. Luce, *AHR* 80 (1975), 944–45; D. R. Shackleton Bailey, *AJPh* 96 (1975), 436–43; M. H. Crawford, *JRS* 66 (1976), 214–17; A. W. Lintott, *CR* 90 (1976), 241–43; D. Stockton, *Gnomon* 49 (1977), 216–18; M. Griffin, *CR* 100 (1986), 271.

21. Cic. *Leg.* 3.20.

22. R. E. Smith, *Service in the Post-Marian Army* (Manchester, 1958). E. Gabba, *Esercito e società nella tarda Repubblica romana* (Florence, 1973), 1–45. The effects of the reform are somewhat downplayed by L. J. F. Keppie, *The Making of the Roman Army* (London, 1984), 61–63.

23. H. Volkmann, *Sullas Marsch auf Rom* (Munich, 1958). B. Levick, "Sulla's March on Rome in 88 B.C.," *Historia* 31 (1982), 503–8.

Chapter Two. From Upstart to "Father of His Country"

1. See Nicolet, "Arpinum, Aemilius Scaurus et les Tullii Cicerones"; also Rawson, "Lucius Crassus and Cicero."

2. For the date, which is in dispute, see E. Badian, *Athenaeum* 34 (1956), 104–23; B. A. Marshall, *Athenaeum* 54 (1976), 117–30; G. V. Sumner, *GRBS* 19 (1978), 147–53. For the exemplary character of his governorship, see F. Münzer, *RE* Mucius (1933), 438–39.

3. Livy *Per.* 111.

4. Mitchell, *Cicero*, 90.

5. Cic. *Att.* 8.3.6.

6. *Iliad* 6.208, 11.784, quoted *QFr.* 3.5.4.

7. *Brut.* 308.

8. *Quinct.* 31. The political aspects of the speech are discussed by Hinard, "Le Pro Quinctio."

9. Sources in Greenidge-Clay, *Sources for Roman History, 133–70* B.C., 2nd ed. (Oxford, 1960), 52.

10. Cic. *De Or.* 3.229; *Brut.* 229. He seems to have spoken twice, on the forum and in the Senate; E. Malcovati, *Oratorum Romanorum Fragmenta*, 2nd ed. (Turin, 1955), 314, n. 1.

11. *Brut.* 308.

12. *Brut.* 311.

13. *Rosc. Am.* 32.

14. I borrowed a phrase from Crawford, *Orations*, 4.

15. See the discussion and bibliography in Broughton, *Magistrates*, 3.74–

75. According to his own testimony, Cicero spoke while Sulla was still in power: "contra L. Sullae dominantis opes" (*Off.* 2.51).

16. See Lloyd W. Daly, "Roman Study Abroad," *AJPh* 71 (1950), 40–58; for Cicero, esp. 46–48.

17. Raubitschek, "Phaidros and His Roman Pupils."

18. For a fuller account, see Gelzer, *Cicero,* 29–70; Mitchell, *Cicero,* 93–176.

19. Cic. *Tusc.* 5.64–66.

20. R. K. Sherk, *Roman Documents from the Greek East* (Baltimore, 1969), 133 f., n. 23, lines 11–12. Almost thirty years later, Cicero used his knowledge of the affair in *Nat. D.* 3.49.

21. Astin, "Cicero and the Censorship."

22. See Payre, "*Homo novus,*" where earlier bibliography is listed; for Caldus, see ibid., p. 60. D. R. Shackleton Bailey, "*Nobiles* and *novi* reconsidered," *AJPh* 107 (1986), 258–60. Vanderbroeck, "*Homo novus* again."

23. *Velleius* 2.34.3: "Marcus Cicero, a man who owed his elevation wholly to himself." For the opposite (inheritance instead of accomplishment), see the remark of M. Antonius about Octavian, who inherited Caesar's name: "And you, o boy . . . you who owe everything to a name" (from a letter to Hirtius and Octavian, quoted by Cicero, *Phil.* 13.24–25).

24. *Fam.* 3.7.5.

25. *Leg. Agr.* 2.100.

26. *Att.* 4.8a.2.

27. *Leg. Agr.* 2.3; *Off.* 2.59.

28. 1. *Verr.* 1.40.

29. Gelzer, *RE* Tullius, 842–52; idem, *Cicero,* 36–50. Stroh, *Taxis und Taktik,* 174–87, argues that Q. Caecilius Niger, against whom Cicero had first to secure the right of representing the plaintiffs (*Div. Caec.*) was not in the least the puppet that Cicero wanted him to appear and may have been, in fact, the Sicilians' first choice.

30. Mommsen's blast against Cicero "thus he came forward in the trial of Verres against the senatorial *judicia* when they were already set aside" (*The History of Rome,* trans. W. P. Dickson [New York, 1894], 4.725) was highly biased, as R. Heinze, "Ciceros politische Anfänge," 112, has shown. Heinze observed that the bill was already promulgated when the trial began, but voted upon only afterwards. It had passed when Cicero wrote the speeches, but his intention was to write as he would have spoken at the trial.

31. I cannot share the view of E. Gruen that the restoration of the tribunician power in 70 B.C. was "innocuous" and did alter the Sullan constitution only slightly in form, not at all in intent (*Last Generation,* 28.46); that view has already been criticized by D. R. Shackleton Bai-

ley, *AJPh* 96 (1975), 439, J.-L. Ferrary, *MEFRA* 87 (1975), 348, and
D. Stockton, *Gnomon* 49 (1977), 217. A. Heuss hardly uses too strong
an expression when he calls the revision of Sulla's constitution a
"Dammbruch" ("Ciceros Theorie," 211). Manilius alone of the tribunes mentioned here did not rise higher in the years following his
tribunate: he was convicted in court, at a time when Pompey, the
beneficiary of his bill, was absent.

32. Q. Cicero, *Commentariolum petitionis.*
33. Cicero's speech "In the white toga," that is, the toga worn by candi-
    dates running for office.
34. Sources in Broughton, *Magistrates,* 2.162.
35. See on this question R. Feger, "T. Pomponius Atticus," *RE* suppl. 8
    (1956), 508–9.
36. Mitchell, *Cicero,* 184–96.
37. *Leg. Agr.* 2.15.
38. *Leg. Agr.* 2.24.
39. *Leg. Agr.* 2.9.
40. See, most recently, Ungern-Sternberg, *Untersuchungen;* Th. Mitchell,
    "Cicero and the Senatus Consultum Ultimum," *Historia* 20 (1971),
    47–61; Bleicken, *Lex publica,* 473–86.
41. He was consul in 71, expelled from the Senate in 70 B.C. and elected
    again as one of the praetors for 63.
42. Sall. *Cat.* 50.3.
43. Cic. *Att.* 12.21 with the notes of D. R. Shackleton Bailey in his edi-
    tion.
44. Cic. *Pis.* 6; *Sest.* 121: *pater patriae.*
45. References in M. Gelzer, *RE* Tullius, 884.
46. References in ibid.
47. See O. Lendle, "Ciceros ὑπόμνημα περὶ τῆς ὑπατείας," 106.
48. Ibid.
49. *Cat.* 3.2.
50. See Ch. Habicht, *Gottmenschentum und griechische Städte,* 2nd ed.
    (Munich, 1970).
51. *De brev. vit.* 5.1.
52. *Rep.* 1.12. See also 6.13: "all those who have preserved, aided, or
    enlarged their fatherland have a special place prepared for them in
    the heavens, where they may enjoy an eternal life of happiness."
53. Cic. *Att.* 1.16.13.
54. Plut. *Cic.* 22.6.

Chapter Three. The Princeps Driven into Exile

1. Meier sees in the year of Cicero's consulship not only the climax but
   also the turning point in his political career ("Ciceros Consulat," 63).

Rawson, *Cicero,* 89: "In a strictly political sense the whole of Cicero's life, hitherto so remarkable a success story, is from this point one of failure."

2. Shackleton Bailey, *Cicero,* 34: "It would have been his apogee, but for that turn of fate which, after twenty years of vanity and vexation, was to present him with a finer hour."

3. Greenidge-Clay, *Sources for Roman History, 133–70* B.C., 2nd ed. (Oxford, 1960), 31–32; for Caesar, Cic. *Cat.* 4.10. Plut. *Cat. min.* 22.5.

4. Cic. *Dom.* 21. For the occasion, probably in 58 B.C., see R. G. Nisbet, *M. Tulli Ciceronis de domo sua ad pontifices oratio* (Oxford, 1939), 86.

5. Cicero himself, however, never changed his dissenting opinion and wrote twenty years later: "for the arrest of guilty men was my duty, their punishment that of the Senate" (*Phil.* 2.18).

6. Cic. *Fam.* 5.2.8.

7. Publication shortly after the events has been very persuasively argued by W. C. McDermott, "Cicero's Publication," 277–84; see also Stroh, *Taxis und Taktik,* 51, n. 90, and Crawford, *Orations,* 79–80, n. 3.

8. *Cat.* 4.10: "But indeed Gaius Caesar knows that the Sempronian law was enacted for Roman citizens; but he also knows that that man cannot possibly be a citizen who is a public enemy of the state." It seems certain that the second part of the sentence was not what Caesar had actually said but was put into his mouth by Cicero.

9. Cicero's theory was accepted, late in life, by Th. Mommsen, *Römisches Strafrecht* (Leipzig, 1899), 256–57. Mommsen is still followed in principle by J. Bleicken, *Savigny-Zeitschr.* 76 (1959), 367, n. 83 (but see below). The fallacy of Cicero's argument has been most clearly exposed by Ch. H. Brecht, *Perduellio* (München, 1938), 72–75, 198–210, 224–26, 250–58. Brecht also discusses (252–53) Cic. *Cat.* 1.28: "But never in this city have those who revolted against the state enjoyed the rights of citizens," but omits to quote (and to discuss) *Cat.* 3.15 (see next note). Brecht's view has been accepted, among others, by H. von Lübtow, *Savigny-Zeitschr.* 61 (1941), 443; H. Siber, ibid., 62 (1942), 390; E. Levy, ibid., 78 (1961), 162 (*Gesammelte Schriften* 2 [Köln and Graz, 1963], 17); M. Kaser, *Jura* 3 (1952), 68, n. 101; Bleicken, *Lex publica,* 475. Different views have since been expressed by Ungern-Sternberg, *Untersuchungen,* 86–129, and by Th. N. Mitchell, "Cicero and the Senatus Consultum Ultimum," *Historia* 20 (1971), 47–61 (see also Mitchell, *Cicero,* 205–19), but have failed to convince me. The proposition that there was a "Doctrine of Manifest Guilt" in the Roman Criminal Law has been laid to rest by Crook, "Was There a 'Doctrine of Manifest Guilt'?" 38–47. For *"hostis domesticus"* and similar hybrid expressions used in this connection, see Jal, "Hostis (publicus) dans la littérature latine," 72–75.

10. Cic. *Cat.* 3.15: "For although Publius Lentulus, in the judgment of

the senate, had lost not only the rights of a praetor, but even the rights of a citizen, after the evidence had been given and he had confessed, still he resigned his office in order that he might suffer punishment as a private citizen." See also *Cat.* 4.5: "You forced Publius Lentulus to resign his praetorship." Sall. *Cat.* 47.3.

11. Sall. *Cat.* 52.25.

12. Sall. *Cat.* 52.36. Cato's own nephew, Marcus Brutus, twenty years after these events, sided with the opinion of Clodius and Caesar against that of Cato and Cicero, since he replied to Cicero's suggestion that he execute his prisoner C. Antonius as follows: "My only conclusion is that the Senate or the People of Rome must pass judgement on those citizens who have not died fighting. You will say that my calling men hostile to the state 'citizens' is an impropriety in itself. On the contrary; it is quite proper. What the Senate has not yet decreed, nor the People ordered, I do not take it upon myself to prejudge, I do not make myself the arbiter" (Cic. *ad Brut.* 1.4.2, of May 43 B.C.). It does not seem to have been noticed that this discussion precisely summarizes the principal arguments of both sides in the debate upon the Catilinarians.

13. For these events, see, e.g., Meyer, *Caesars Monarchie,* 37–41; M. Gelzer, *RE* Tullius, 891–93.

14. He even participated, together with Quintus Hortensius, in the defense of Publius Sulla accused of complicity in Catilina's schemes. Sulla was acquitted, but rumor had it that Cicero, even before the verdict, had received two million sesterces from him, which allowed him to buy a splendid house on the Palatine from Crassus. The point is that fees for lawyers were illegal in Rome. It was also said that Cicero defended others similarly indicted, if they paid him, but testified against those unable, or unwilling, to pay. It is difficult to assess the truth of those accusations; in any event, the story about the payoff from Sulla has the ring of authenticity.

15. Cic. *Cat.* 3.26.

16. *Fam.* 5.7.3.

17. *Att.* 1.19.7; 2.1.6, both from the spring of 60 B.C.

18. *Att.* 2.17.2. Sampsiceramus (or Sampsigeramus) was an Arabian dynast of Emesa (Homs) in Syria with whom Pompey had some dealings in 63 B.C. Cicero used his name as a nickname for Pompey in those times he was at odds with him.

19. *Att.* 10.4.4.

20. *Fam.* 1.8.3. It may have been this passage which induced Eduard Schwartz to write: "He wanted nothing more than to show off with his speeches and be useful to his country" ("Cicero," 100).

21. See Meier, "Die Ersten unter den Ersten des Senats," esp. 196–98.

22. Cic. *Att.* 1.13.2: the consul is "of petty and perverse mentality."

23. The point is well made in Martin, "Cicéron Princeps," 850–78 (whose overall assessment of Cicero differs from mine).
24. For Torquatus, see Cic. *Sull.* 21–22, 25; for Clodius, Cic. *Att.* 1. 16.10. Other instances are found in Bleicken, *Lex publica,* 478, n. 340, who explains these expressions as allusions to the fact that Cicero as consul had violated the civic rights of the Catilinarians by denying them the right to a trial.
25. See the instructive analysis, discussing all the *viri consulares* of the time, by Parrish, "The Senate on January 1, 62 B.C.." Her conclusion (168) is: "Cicero . . . was in a uniquely influential position in 62."
26. *Att.* 7.3.2. The hope for a triumph was an impediment, since Cicero, who returned as *imperator* from his province, could not enter the city without losing the *imperium* which was a requirement for the triumph. By staying outside the city, he kept it, but was thereby debarred from any major political role. Caesar had once faced a similar dilemma, when returning from Spain in 60 B.C.; he gave up the triumph in order to secure his nomination for the consular election.
27. *Att.* 1.20.3.
28. See Badian, *Publicans and Sinners,* 100–101.
29. *Att.* 2.1.6. While Pompey is here accused of "levitas popularis" (courting popularity with the masses), it will later be Caesar, who, according to Cicero in his fifth Philippic (49), "has wasted all his unique ability in it," "omnem vim ingeni, quae summa fuit in illo, in populari levitate consumpsit."
30. Ibid.
31. On the significance of the title, see Astbury, "Varro and Pompey."
32. *Att.* 2.7.4.
33. *Att.* 2.3.4.
34. Cic. *Pis.* 73–74; *Off.* 1.77. In W. Miller's translation: "Yield, ye arms, to the toga, to civic praises, ye laurels," where the reading is *laudi* instead of *linguae.*
35. *Att.* 2.16.2.
36. Cic. *Dom.* 41. With regard to Clodius's wish to become a plebeian, see the observation of W. M. Lindsay, *The Latin Language* (Oxford, 1894), 41: "Cicero's rival Clodius was the first of the gens to change the name *Claudius* to *Clodius,* no doubt with the view of conciliating the mob."
37. Plutarch's story (*Cic.* 29.2–3) that the enmity, in fact, originated in the hatred that Cicero's wife Terentia felt for Clodius and his sister Clodia, although rejected by most scholars, has recently found an advocate in Epstein, "Cicero's Testimony."
38. *Att.* 1.9.1, with Shackleton Bailey's remark: "he is whistling rather stridently in the dark."
39. Livy *Per.* 103: "Marcus Cicero was sent into exile by a law passed by

Publius Clodius as tribune of the commons, on the charge of having put citizens to death without a trial." *Velleius* 2.45.1: "Publius Clodius . . . as tribune, proposed a law that whoever put to death a Roman citizen without trial should be condemned to exile." For the *lex Clodia*, see Moreau, "La lex Clodia"; for the events of the years 58 and 57, see Grimal, *Études de chronologie cicéronienne*.

40. As Cicero enumerates (*QFr.* 1.4.4): "Pompey's sudden desertion, the unfriendly attitude of the Consuls, and even the Praetors, the timidity of the tax-farmers, the sight of weapons."

41. Cic. *Dom.* 47.50–51. The question put to the voters was, "That it may please you, that you may command, that Marcus Tullius be interdicted from fire and water" (ibid., 47). The reason given for the intended punishment was that, as consul, "Cicero had reported on a falsified decree of the Senate" (ibid., 50), on the strength of which citizens had been executed. Such an accusation was first made in 62 by Torquatus during the trial of P. Sulla (Cic. *Sull.* 40–46). It was most certainly unfounded; one of the four senators appointed to record the proceedings word for word had been Clodius's own brother, Appius Claudius Pulcher; see Gabba, "Cicerone." Th. N. Mitchell has argued (*Historia* 20 [1971], 61) that if falsification were the issue, the decree itself which authorized the execution of the Catilinarians would thereby be tacitly acknowledged as a legal instrument. This is hardly convincing; Clodius apparently made use of an older accusation in order to isolate Cicero from his peers in the Senate and to shake the solidarity of the senators with their former leader, who alone was singled out as being accountable.

42. Cicero himself admits that he has lost his citizenship, if the second *lex Clodia* were, in fact, a valid law (*Att.* 3.23.2).

43. So did L. Aurelius Cotta, consul for 65 B.C. (Cic. *Sest.* 73; *Leg.* 3.45), P. Cornelius Lentulus, cos. 57 (Cic. *Red. Sen.* 8), and Q. Terentius Culleo, *trib. pl.* 58 (Cic. *Att.* 3.15.5).

44. Cic. *Red. Sen.* 26 being the most explicit of several passages.

45. Shackleton Bailey, *Cicero*, xii.

46. *Att.* 3.7.2; 8.4; 10.2; 13.2; 15.2.

47. *Att.* 3.3; 4; 7.2; *Fam.* 14.4.5.

48. *Att.* 3.7.2; 15.6; 6; 19.1; 26. *QFr.* 1.3.6; 1.4.4.

49. *Att.* 3.10.2; 15.2; 22.3.

50. *Att.* 3.10.1; 13.2.

51. *Att.* 3.8.4; 14.1; 15.4; 20.1.

52. *Att.* 3.9.2. *QFr.* 1.3.8.

53. *Att.* 3.8.2; 9.2; 10.2; 13.2; 19.3; 20.1. *Fam.* 14.1.1. *QFr* 1.3.5; 1.4.1–2. See above, n. 35.

54. *Att.* 3.15.2.

55. *Att.* 3.9.1; 15.4; 15.7.

56. *Att.* 3.15.6; 23.5; 24.1; 25; 27.
57. Sen. *Suas.* 6.24.
58. B. Niebuhr, *Lebensnachrichten* 2 (Hamburg, 1838), 483, as quoted by P. Groebe (Drumann, 2nd ed., 6.xi).
59. Cic. *Att.* 2.18.3. As Kumaniecki (*Cicerone,* 17) observed, he turned down, from 60 to 56, all offers from the triumvirs. See also Rawson, *Cicero,* 106: "it was from shame and principle alone that he stood out of the alliance."
60. In 1969, M. Gelzer added a significant new page to what he had written many years earlier (*RE* Tullius 905) in his *Cicero,* 121–22. He writes that Cicero's refusal in 60/59 B.C. to cooperate with Caesar caused his political activity thereafter to be doomed to failure. He adds: "Instinct for power might have let him to perceive that it was time to leave the sinking ship of the *principes* for the triumvirate, if he still wished to play an effective role in politics." This view is shared by E. Gruen (*AJPh* 91 [1970], 236): "The instinct for power inherent in a natural born politician was lacking in Cicero," and by Meier ("Ciceros Consulat," 115): "man ignorant of power." It is unanswerable as far as Cicero's ability to affect the course of events is concerned. But there is also another dimension to this. As R. Seager has remarked (*JRS* 60 [1970], 213), "it is doubtful whether a developed *Machtinstinkt* was compatible with Cicero's conception of a *princeps civitatis* or indeed anything that Cicero would have acknowledged as *res publica* at all." See also R. G. Nisbet, *M. Tulli Ciceronis de domo sua ad pontifices oratio* (Oxford, 1939), xvi: "Cicero stood firm until he was broken."
61. See on this most recently J. Glucker, "As Has Been Rightly Said."
62. Cic. *QFr.* 1.4.4: "Pompey's sudden desertion."
63. See on this Balsdon, "Roman History 58–56 B.C.," 16–18.
64. Cic. *QFr.* 2.1.1, where the words "There were . . . some complaints to Pompey's address—who was not present" perhaps indicate that the speaker wanted to dissociate himself from Pompey.
65. *Vat.* 15.36–37.
66. *Fam.* 1.9.8–10.
67. It is a matter of dispute how dangerous the threat to Caesar really was and whether Cicero played a leading role in the scheme (M. Cary, *CQ* 17 [1923], 103–7, followed by most other scholars), or only a supporting one (Th. N. Mitchell, *TAPA* 100 [1969], 295–320; see also Gruen, *Last Generation,* 100, n. 46). However that may be, the fact remains that Caesar immediately reacted and that he complained about Cicero's activity in the matter, with the result that Cicero, when the question was discussed in the Senate on the day he himself had proposed, abstained from attending the meeting and felt constrained to remain silent, as he wrote to his brother (*QFr.* 2.7.2): "On this

matter I am muzzled," as Shackleton Bailey, *Cicero*, 83, translates the phrase, for which see also his note in his edition of the letter. See also the discussion quoted in Crawford, *Orations*, 155, n. 12, from *LCM* 5.5–5.8 (1980).

68. See Ward, "Conference of Luca."
69. See Ruebel, "When Did Cicero Learn about the Conference at Luca?": "On or about 25 April 56."

Chapter Four. *"Good night to principle, sincerity, and honor"*

1. *Fam.* 1.7.7.
2. *Fam.* 1.9.21. Gelzer, *Cicero*, 133 and n. 219.
3. *Fam.* 1.7.10, where impersonal wording is used to hide the fact that Cicero himself had moved for acceptance—clearly a sign of an uneasy conscience. He admitted this later in another letter to the same addressee who, at that time, knew it anyway, *Fam.* 1.9.17.
4. *Fam.* 1.7.10 and, above all, the entire speech *De provinciis consularibus*.
5. Kumaniecki, *Cicerone*, 323, rightly observes that Cicero's attempts to extenuate the facts were in vain; it was all too obvious that he had passed from the camp of the nobility into that of the dynasts and that he now assisted those whom he had so far opposed.
6. As Shackleton Bailey puts it (*Cicero's Letters* [1965], 2.184): "But his complaints can hardly be more than a smoke-screen for the true reason of his recantation, namely the danger of opposing the coalition just re-established at Luca after Pompey's plain warning. C. did not want to go on his travels again."
7. There was, in fact, for some time an alliance between the *boni* and Clodius, directed against Pompey, which understandably infuriated Cicero (Rundell, "Cicero and Clodius," 328).
8. *Fam.* 1.7.10: "The party superior in resources, armed force, and power has actually contrived, so it seems to me, to gain moral ascendancy as well" ("qui plus opibus, armis, potentia valent, perfecisse tamen mihi videntur . . . ut etiam auctoritate iam plus valerent").
9. *Att.* 4.5.1. It is not entirely certain that he alludes to the speech on the consular provinces (see Balsdon, "Roman History 65–50 B.C.," 137–39).
10. *Att.* 4.6.2.
11. *JRS* 60 (1970), 213, also quoted with approval by A. E. Douglas, *JRS* 62 (1972), 229. See further Mittelstadt, "Cicero's Political *Velificatio Mutata.*" In the summer of 54 B.C., Cicero had to defend himself against the charge "that my liberty of action has been curtailed because I am no longer at variance with all those with whom I was once at variance" (*Planc.* 91). The accusation was made by Marcus Juven-

tius Laterensis, a staunch republican, who had helped Cicero and his family during Cicero's exile and who would take his own life in 43 B.C., when his commander Lepidus betrayed the Senate, led at the time by Cicero, and joined forces with Antonius (see F. Münzer, *RE* Iuventius [1919], 1365–67).

12. Cic. *Fam.* 7.1.4: "sometimes I am obliged to defend persons who have deserved none too well of me, at the request of those who *have* deserved well."

13. Cic. *Fam.* 1.9.4; 19–20.

14. Fantham, "The Trials of Gabinius in 54 B.C."; Crawford, *Orations*, 188–97.

15. *QFr.* 3.1.15.

16. Stockton, *Cicero*, 215.

17. Ps. Sallust, *In M. Tullium Ciceronem Invectiva*, passim, esp. 7.

18. *QFr.* 3.5.4: "Some of my enemies I have refrained from attacking, others I have actually defended. My mind, even my animosities, are in chains." In this connection, Shackleton Bailey remarks: "In spite of such passages (written perhaps in part as a sop to his own conscience) Cicero's early fifties ought not to be regarded as one of the bleaker periods in his life. On the whole he was probably less unhappy than at any time subsequent to his Consulship. The tone of his letters is prevailingly cheerful, even gay" (*Cicero*, 88). The question is, of course, whether the gay or the somber tones reflect Cicero's basic mood. I cannot help taking most of the cheerful expressions as forced and superficial. As he kindly informed me, Shackleton Bailey continues to disagree and thinks my psychology is wrong here.

19. Meier, "Ciceros Consulat," 115: Cicero the politician not on a par with himself in other respects.

20. Cic. *QFr.* 2.8.3: "The fact is, they are all-powerful and want everybody to know it."

21. On this work and its sequence, the *De legibus*, see the fine chapter "Cicero on the Republic," in Rawson's *Cicero*, 146–63 and her verdict (159): "Whatever the shortcomings of Cicero's political works, there is no evidence that any of his contemporaries understood the problems of the time as clearly or indeed produced nearly so positive a contribution towards solving them as he did." The enormous bibliography is discussed by Schmidt, "Cicero *De re publica*." Among earlier works, outstanding is Heinze, "Ciceros *Staat* als politische Tendenzschrift." On the third book of *De legibus*, see the thorough analysis of Heuss, "Ciceros Theorie vom römischen Staat."

22. There are perceptive remarks on how the writing affected his mentality by Schwartz ("Cicero," 105) and Meier ("Cicero," 189). Fuhrmann observes that it was during these years that Cicero became "Rome's greatest political thinker" ("Cum dignitate otium," 481).

23. K. Büchner, *RE* Tullius, 1256. Cicero had visited Caesar in the winter of 53/52 B.C. in Ravenna (*Att.* 7.1.4, with Shackleton Bailey's note): "he agreed to use his influence to ensure that Caelius Rufus, Tribune in 52, did not oppose the *privilegium*" (Caesar's right to register his candidacy for another consulship *in absentia,* while he was still in Gaul).
24. *Fam.* 1.9.20; *Att.* 4.13.2: "what a rascal he is!" See also *Off.* 3.73 (on Hortensius and Crassus): "Although I loved the one while he lived and do not hate the other now that he is dead."
25. See the sources, especially Dio Cassius and Plutarch, in Crawford, *Orations,* 213–18. Dio's treatment of Cicero is assessed by F. Millar, *A Study of Cassius Dio* (Oxford, 1964), 46–55, with this summary: "Dio's handling of Cicero is a failure, perhaps the most complete failure of his History."
26. This is also stressed by A. W. Lintott, *CR* 88 (1974), 67. Asconius comments as follows (p. 38 Clark, trans. N. H. Watts): "So great, however, was Cicero's resolution and loyalty that neither by the estrangement of the people from himself, nor by the suspicion of Pompeius, not by the fear of danger to come, should he be arraigned before the people, nor by the arms openly wielded against Milo, could he be deterred from his defence, although he might have avoided all danger to himself and the hatred of the embittered populace, nay, have even won back Pompeius's favour, had he abated but a little in his ardour for the defence." See also B. A. Marshall, *A Historical Commentary on Asconius* (Columbia, Mo., 1985), 190–91.
27. Crawford, *Orations,* 219–21 (Saufeius); 230–34 (Munatius). Cicero's triumphant mood: *Fam.* 7.2.2–3. Stone remarks ("Pro Milone," 108): "Not since before the conference of Luca had Cicero held so splendid, so independent a position in public life. His elation appears in a letter to M. Marius" (this is *Fam.* 7.2.2–3). The victim, as so many others in similar circumstances, found shelter and a new career at Caesar's headquarters.
28. Girardet, "Die Lex Iulia de provinciis," 293–300.
29. So Stockton, *Cicero,* 244. This, as so many other derogatory statements, goes back to Mommsen, who wrote that Cicero did not so much abhor injustice itself as its exposure, and that he did not care for integrity, but only for the reputation of integrity (*Hermes* 24 [1899], 147, in a paper on Brutus as a loan shark). Similarly, Shackleton Bailey, *Cicero,* 114: "Fame, not philanthropy or the beauty of virtue, was Cicero's spur." The thought is expressed by Cicero himself as follows: "For many wish not so much to be, as to seem to be, endowed with real virtue" (*Amic.* 98). It does not follow that he was guilty of the charge. Cicero was, indeed, sensitive of his reputation, and concern for it certainly contributed to his conduct, but the letters

show concern for his subjects, too. H. Kasten also takes issue with Shackleton Bailey in this matter (*Gymnasium* 74 [1967], 166). A. E. Douglas's assessment seems right to me: "Cicero's provincial administration and his handling of the Scaptius affair in particular (this is the affair discussed by Mommsen) represent a standard far above that of almost all of his contemporaries—so far, one may conclude, as to justify the pride in his conduct" (*g & r*, new surveys 2 [1968], 2). See also Schwartz, "Cicero," 105: "there can be no doubt that he governed with as much humanity and integrity as was possible under the corrupt rule of the senate and the capitalists." Most recently, Rauh, "Cicero's Business Friendships," 21–30.

30. Cic. *Fam.* 8.1–14. Cicero's letters to Caelius are *Fam.* 2.8–15.

31. Deroux, "L'identité de Lesbie." A different opinion in Stroh, *Taxis und Taktik*, 296–98.

32. See, e.g., the chapter "The Coming of Civil War," in Gruen's *Last Generation*, 449–97 (where, however, the sentence of Cic. *Fam.* 8.8.9: "These utterances . . . have produced an impression that Pompey is having trouble with Caesar" [469 with n. 70] is misunderstood; see D. R. Shackleton Bailey, *AJPh* 96 [1975], 440). More recently, Giovannini, *Consulare Imperium*, 103–46.

33. Caelius: *Fam.* 8.14.2. Cicero: *Att.* 6.8.2; 9.5; cf. *Fam.* 14.5.1.

34. Cic. *Att.* 7.1.3.

35. *Att.* 8.1.3; 3.2–3; 9.3; 14.2; 15.2; 9.1.3; 4.2; *Div.* 1.27; 2.78–79. Cicero repeated as much after Caesar's victory in Caesar's presence (*Lig.* 19): "today that course must be adjudged the better whereto the gods added their assistance." Similarly already *Marcell.* 16: "it is not cause with cause that we must compare today, but victory with victory." On the other hand, while he was in Pompey's camp, he found fault with almost everything, so that he later (spring 46 B.C.) wrote to a friend: "In a phrase, nothing good except the cause" (*Fam.* 7.3.2.). In retrospect: "that war in which the one side was too prolific in crime, the other in failure" (*Off.* 2.45).

36. *Att.* 7.3.5.

37. *Att.* 7.3.4; 5.5; 6.2.

38. *Att.* 6.8.2. See, however, Shackleton Bailey's note (*Cicero's Letters*, [1968] 3.274): speculation, rather, that Pompey might leave Rome to take over his province in Spain from his lieutenants.

39. *Att.* 5.6.2.

40. *Att.* 7.8.5.

41. *Att.* 7.7.7.

42. *Att.* 7.3.4. See Bringmann, *Untersuchungen*, 18–19. Kumaniecki, *Cicerone*, 17–18.

43. *Att.* 7.5.4; 8.11.2: "both want to reign." 9.7.1; 10.4.4; 7.1: "this is a fight for a throne." See also *Brut.* 329; *Tusc.* 3.4.

44. *Att.* 7.5.4.
45. *Att.* 7.14.3; 8.11 D.6; *Fam.* 6.6.5; 16.12.2; *Off.* 1.35; *Phil.* 2.37.
46. Cic. *Fam.* 8.14.3; *Att.* 7.3.6. Cicero would thus comment after Caelius's death (*Brut.* 273): "but to my sorrow after my departure he fell away from his own past standards, and . . . brought about his own fall."
47. *Att.* 7.12.3.
48. *Att.* 7.11.1: "And he says he is doing all this for his honour's sake! Where is honour without moral good?" ("ubi est autem dignitas nisi ubi honestas?")
49. Caes. *BCiv.* 1.7.7; 9.2. Cf. Cic. *Lig.* 18; *Deiot.* 11. See Raaflaub, *Dignitatis Contentio,* esp. 149 ff., 181 ff.
50. Cic. *Lig.* 33; *Att.* 9.10.2.
51. His report to Pompey of 15 February 49 B.C. (*Att.* 8.11 B) reveals his incompetence. He himself admits to Atticus that he has done little, *Att.* 8.3.4–5. See further Appendix 2, "Cicero's Command in 49" in 4.438–40, of Shackleton Bailey's *Cicero's Letters.*
52. *Att.* 8.1.3; 3.2–3; 9.3–4; 14.2; 15.2: "To stay is certainly the more prudent course, to go overseas is thought the more honourable." *Fam.* 4.2.2. Strasburger (*Caesar,* 42–43) expresses well his tribulations when he remarks that Cicero, a man all too often superficial and rash, now really struggled and that the conflict is reflected in his soul as if *he himself* were the soul of the Republic. For all of this, see now with a much fuller presentation of the evidence, Brunt's detailed study "Cicero's *Officium* in the Civil War," published after the above had been written.
53. *Att.* 8.11 D.3–4.
54. *Att.* 9.10.2; 10.8.5. The passage is very characteristic of Cicero: "I did not go abroad with Pompey; true, I did not have the opportunity—the dates are there to prove it. Still—I may as well acknowledge what is the fact—I did not try very hard to give myself the opportunity. One thing misled me, perhaps it ought not to have done but it did: I thought there would be peace."
55. Cic. *Att.* 9.17.1.
56. *Att.* 9.18.
57. *Att.* 10.8 B (Caesar's letter of April 16); 10.8 A (letter of Marcus Antonius). Antonius was instructed not to let him (or any other person of rank) leave: 10.10.
58. They were Servius Sulpicius Rufus, cos. 51, and Gaius Marcellus, cos. 50: *Att.* 10.14.1; 14.3; 15.2.
59. *Fam.* 14.7.2. See also *Fam.* 7.3.2 of April 46 to Marcus Marius: "I preferred to yield to the claims of honour and reputation than to calculate for my own safety."
60. Plut. *Cic.* 38.1. "It is interesting to find this subsequent justification

of Cicero's sluggish course in the winter, which some modern scholars have stigmatized as treason to the state" (Rawson, *Cicero*, 199).
61. *Fam.* 7.3.2.
62. *Fam.* 9.9.
63. Caes. *BCiv.* 3.62–72.
64. Cic. *Att.* 11.7.2.
65. Cic. *Att.* 11.7.3.
66. *Att.* 11.12.3; 19.1; 24.5.
67. *Att.* 11.15.2; 25.1.
68. *Att.* 11.14.1.
69. Cic. *Fam.* 14.23. The battle has become famous by Caesar's remark,
"veni, vidi, vici" (Suet. *Iul.* 37; cf. Plut. *Caes.* 50).

Chapter Five. Liberty Recovered and Lost

1. Plut. *Cat. Min.* 66.2. Concerning the pardons granted by Caesar after
Pharsalus, Cicero wrote to Atticus on 15 August 47 B.C.: "and Caesar's
concessions, from a master to slaves, are his to revoke at will" (*Att.*
11.20.1).
2. A. Heuss, *HZ* 237 (1985), 91.
3. Alföldi, *Caesar in 44 v. Chr.*, 173–386.
4. Soon after the events it became commonplace that Cato, with his
death, had scored a moral victory, for which Lucan's verse has become the classic expression: "If the victor had the gods on his side,
the vanquished had Cato" ("victrix causa deis placuit sed victa Ca-
toni," *Pharsalia* 1.128). Cicero had already come close to saying the
same thing (*Lig.* 19). See also Griffin, "Philosophy, Cato, and Roman
Suicide," 194 ff.
5. *Fam.* 9.2.4–5.
6. *Fam.* 9.17.2.
7. *Fam.* 13.68.2. See also 12.17.1.
8. Cic. *Marcell.* 24–27. See the comments of Bringmann, *Untersuchungen*, 75–76; Dahlmann, "Cicero, Caesar und der Untergang," 347–48;
Cipriani, "La Pro Marcello."
9. *Fam.* 6.21.2.
10. *Fam.* 6.1.4.
11. Cic. *Fam.* 9.20.1; *Tusc.* 1.1.; *Off.* 3.2.
12. *Fam.* 4.9.2.
13. Cic. *Fam.* 6.8.1. Malitz, "Die Kanzlei Caesars."
14. *Fam.* 9.16.3.
15. Bringmann, "Der Diktator Caesar," has clarified the circumstances of
these two speeches; there were no legal proceedings. When, in May
45, Gaius Marius, an impostor who pretended to be a grandson of
the great Marius, called on Cicero to undertake his defense, Cicero

replied "that he had no need of an advocate, since his excellent and generous kinsman Caesar was all-powerful" (*Att.* 12.49.2).

16. *Fam.* 9.18.1: *regnum forense.*

17. Cicero reflects on what his *dignitas* could be under the prevailing conditions in *Fam.* 4.14.1 (winter 46/45 B.C.).

18. *Fam.* 4.13.6: "I shall both cultivate his intimates, who have no small regard for me and are much in my company, and find a way into familiar intercourse with himself, from which a sense of shame on my part has deterred me hitherto." Cicero's principal activity of that kind can be dated to the months from August to December 46 B.C. Nearly all the pertinent letters can be found in books 6 and 4 of the correspondence with his friends.

19. Göttingen, 1971. See the reviews of A. E. Douglas, *JRS* 65 (1975), 198–200, and of M. Ruch, *Rev.phil.* 47 (1973), 103–8.

20. Bringmann, *Untersuchungen,* 17.

21. *Fam.* 4.13.2: "my troubles are such that I feel guilty in continuing to live." *Att.* 13.28.2: "to be alive at all is a disgrace for me."

22. *Att.* 12.4.2. The tenor of the lost pamphlet may be inferred from passages such as *Tusc.* 1.74; 5.4; *Fin.* 4.44 (Cato "that pattern of all the virtues"); 4.61; *Off.* 1.112; 3.66. On Cicero's *Cato,* see, recently, Jones, "Cicero's *Cato*"; Kumaniecki, "Ciceros *Cato*"; Kierdorf, "Ciceros *Cato*"; Zecchini, "La morte di Catone."

23. Cic. *Att.* 12.41.4: "the abuse of Cato which Caesar has written"; 44.1: "these people's abuse" where the plural indicates both Hirtius's and Caesar's pamphlets. Tschiedel, *Caesars 'Anticato,'* has tried to exonerate Caesar in this matter, with limited success.

24. See W. Kroll in W. S. Teuffel, *Geschichte der Römischen Literatur,* 6th ed. (Leipzig and Berlin, 1916) 1.529–30 (where Fadius Gallus must be emended to Fabius Gallus; contra, Tschiedel, *Caesars 'Anticato,'* 11, n. 41). While Cato was still alive, Metellus Pius had published a polemical pamphlet against him (Plut. *Cat.Min.* 57.3, Pliny, *HN* 8.196; 29.96).

25. *Fam.* 6.6.10: "He never mentions Pompey's name except in the most respectful terms."

26. Tschiedel, *Caesars 'Anticato,'* 17, concludes that Caesar, while always respecting Cicero as an equal, used to treat Cato condescendingly.

27. *Att.* 13.31.3. The text continues: "That we shall manage by holding our tongues and lying low."

28. *Att.* 13.40.1.

29. He did so several times in the early months of the Civil War, 49 B.C.: *Att.* 7.11.1; 8.11.2; 10.7.1; 8.7. For earlier (and later) instances in Cicero and other contemporary writers, see Allen, "Caesar's *Regnum.*"

30. *Fam.* 4.8.2, August 46 B.C.

31. *Att.* 13.37.2; *Fam.* 6.19.2, both from August 45 B.C. It has been ob-

served long ago that these two passages are the earliest in which Cicero calls Caesar the dictator *rex* (Tyrrell and Purser, *Correspondence,* 2nd ed., 5.173; Allen, "Caesar's *Regnum,*" 235, n. 13).

32. *Fam.* 11.27.8 in his letter to C. Matius, written some months after Caesar's murder: "if Caesar was a despot *(rex),* which seems to me to be the case."

33. *Att.* 13.40.1 (17 August 45 B.C.): "So what becomes of that work of art of yours which I saw in the Parthenon—Ahala and Brutus?" For C. Servilius Ahala, see F. Münzer, *RE* Servilius, no. 32 (1923), 1768–71; Broughton, *Magistrates,* 1.56. As Münzer observed (1771), Cicero had already made a similar appeal in 59 B.C., directed against Pompey's excessive power (*Att.* 2.24.3, with Shackleton Bailey's note *Cicero's Letters,* 2.402).

34. *Tusc.* 4.1–2; 4.50; *Fin.* 2.66. References to Ahala and Brutus occur also in *Sen.* 56 (Ahala) and 75 (Brutus) of 45/44 B.C. and in *Amic.* 28 of October/November 44 B.C. For Harmodius and Aristogiton, see *Tusc.* 1.116. As J. E. King remarks in his edition of *Tusc.* (382, n. 1): "Every now and again there are hints of what was expected of Marcus Brutus in regard to Caesar."

35. Same conclusion in Collins, "Caesar and the Corruption of Power," 450: "the plainly expressed wish for Caesar's death." Meier, "Cicero," 211: "no question for him that Caesar had to be assassinated. He also admonished Brutus to do it." See also Meier, *Caesar,* 542–43. Cic. *Att.* 12.45.2 (cf. 13.28.3): "I prefer to have him sharing a temple with Quirinus rather than with Weal" is perhaps another expression of the same wish; see A. D. Nock, *HSCP* 41 (1930), 1 f. with n. 1; Meyer, *Caesars Monarchie,* 449; Holleman, "Cicero's Reaction to the Julian Calendar," 498; St. Borszák, "Cicero und Caesar," 34 and works cited there; but see Rossi, "Bruto, Cicerone," and the skeptical note of Shackleton Bailey, *Cicero's Letters,* 5.338. In the light of the other passages, however, there is little room for the doubts expressed by Rawson, *Cicero,* 257: "The pressure on Brutus to emulate his ancestors was apparently becoming intense; there is no reason to think that Cicero joined in it." Her view seems to be based on the anonymous messages recorded by Plutarch and Cassius Dio.

36. H. Strasburger, "Ciceros philosophisches Spätwerk als Aufruf gegen die Herrschaft Caesars," unpublished paper delivered on 15 April 1978 before the Academy at Heidelberg.

37. See the summary in *Jahrbuch der Heidelberger Akademie der Wissenschaften für das Jahr 1978,* 38–40; the quotation is from p. 39: "a large-scale assault upon Caesar's rule."

38. For Torquatus, see F. Münzer, *RE* Manlius (1928), 1203–7; for Triarius, H. Volkmann, *RE* Valerius (1955), 234; for Piso, see R. Syme, *CP* 50 (1955), 134–35, who distinguished father and son, thereby

superseding H. Gundel, *RE* Pupius (1959), 1987–93. This was kindly brought to my attention by D. R. Shackleton Bailey. The deaths of Torquatus, Triarius, and other good men and true were already lamented by both Cicero and Marcus Brutus in *Brut.* 265–66, early spring 46 B.C. In this connection B. Kytzler (*Cicero, Brutus,* 2nd ed. [Munich, 1977], 277) remarks: "One of the trails that lead to the Ides of March begins in Cicero's *Brutus.*"

39. W. Kroll, *RE* Nigidius (1936), 200–12.

40. Meyer, *Caesars Monarchie,* 438–44; R. Philippson, *RE* Tullius (1939), 1134–35. Gelzer, *Cicero,* 315–16. Tschiedel, *Caesars 'Anticato',* 41–44, has a good discussion of this.

41. *Att.* 13.27.1.

42. *Att.* 13.28.2.

43. *Att.* 13.44.1. Gelzer, *Cicero,* 316.

44. This is best illustrated by Cicero's report on Caesar's visit in December 45 B.C., *Att.* 13.52. See the comments of Dahlmann, "Cicero, Caesar und der Untergang," 350–51.

45. For his acts, see M. Gelzer, *Caesar: Politician and Statesman,* trans. P. Needham (Cambridge, Mass., 1968), 308–28; for his public remarks, Suet. *Iul.* 77: "No less arrogant were his public utterances, which Titus Ampius records: that the state was nothing, a mere name without body or form, that Sulla did not know his A.B.C. when he laid down his dictatorship; that men ought now to be more circumspect in addressing him, and to regard his word as law."

46. Cic. *Phil.* 2.28.30. "For the large public his name was the symbol of the Republic, not of this or that party" (Schwartz, "Cicero," 111).

47. *Phil.* 2.25: "that Caesar was slain by my advice." See also 28. It has often been stated, for instance by Meyer, *Caesars Monarchie,* 457, that there was some truth in the accusation.

48. *Rep.* 2.46: "L. Brutus . . . only a private citizen . . . was the first in our State to demonstrate that no one is a mere private citizen when the liberty of his fellows needs protection." He would later insist that to kill a tyrant is the most noble of all glorious deeds (*Off.* 3.19, cf. 3.32).

49. Ch. Habicht, *Chiron* 6 (1976), 141–42, where the evidence is collected.

50. Bailey, *Cicero,* 228. For Cicero's motto, see *Iliad* 6.208, 11.784 as quoted in *QFr* 3.5.4.

51. Cic. *Phil.* 1.1; cf. *Phil.* 5.30: "ieci . . . fundamenta rei publicae."

52. Cic. *Phil.* 2.1: "in these twenty years there was never an enemy of the Commonwealth who did not at the same time declare war on me."

53. Cic. *Red. Sen.* 34. He again expressed the opinion that in 57 B.C. the fate of the state depended on his recall from exile in 56 (*Sest.* 87) and still in 44 (*Off.* 2.58: "the country, whose preservation then depended

upon my recall from exile.") See also Glucker, "As Has Been Rightly Said," 6–9.

54. Cic. *Phil.* 8.27.
55. M. Brutus, in Cic. *ad Brut.* 1.16.5.
56. *Att.* 16.15.6. Stockton, *Cicero,* 300.
57. Cic. *De off.* 3.121. Glucker, "As Has Been Rightly Said," 6–9.
58. For the status of Octavian and his army between October and December 44, see Linderski, "Rome, Aphrodisias and the *Res Gestae,*" 78–79.
59. It has generally been held that on 28 November Antonius had the provinces held by Brutus, Cassius, and Trebonius assigned to new governors, thereby cancelling the agreement of 17 March with Caesar's assassins and opening hostilities against them (W. Sternkopf, *Hermes* 47 [1912], 321–401, esp. 395–97, followed by M. Gelzer, R. Syme, and others). In a few brilliant pages, W. Stroh has destroyed the grounds for that view. It is almost certain that Antonius did no such thing and that Brutus's activities in Macedonia were not prompted by his actions but by Cicero's motions adopted by the Senate on 20 December 44 ("Die Provinzverlosung"). Stroh has also shown that Cicero's speech of 20 December, the third *Philippic,* was, strictly speaking, the first of the cycle ("Ciceros demosthenische Redezyklen"); see also Ch. Schäublin, *MH* 45 (1988), 60–61.
60. Bleicken, *Lex publica,* 491–508. See also Bellincioni, *Cicerone,* 87–97.
61. *Res gestae* 1: "annos undeviginti natus exercitum privato consilio et privata impensa comparavi, per quem rem publicam a dominatione factionis oppressam in libertatem vindicavi."
62. *Phil.* 3.3–5: "C. Caesar adulescens . . . exercitum . . . comparavit patrimoniumque suum effudit . . . qua peste privato consilio rem publicam liberavit." See Béranger, "Cicéron précurseur politique," 128–34; Braunert, "Zum Eingangssatz."
63. Tac. *Ann.* 1.10.1: "cupidine dominandi concitos per largitionem veteranos, paratum ab adulescente privato exercitum, corruptas consulis legiones."
64. Cic. *Fam.* 11.20.1, a letter of Decimus Brutus to Cicero.
65. *Fam.* 10.28.2: "de tota re publica."
66. R. Feger, "Titus Pomponius Atticus," *RE* suppl. 9 (1956), 514.
67. *ad Brut.* 2.5.2: "nisi Caesari Octaviano deus quidam illam mentem dedisset."
68. *Phil.* 5.23: "sua sponte . . . tamen approbatione auctoritatis meae."
69. *Phil.* 5.43: "hunc divinum adulescentem."
70. *Phil.* 5.30: "ieci fundamenta rei publicae." *Fam.* 12.25.2; in an impersonal manner, *Phil.* 6.2, and *Phil.* 4.1. See also *Fam.* 10.28.2.
71. *Phil.* 14.20: "princeps revocandae libertatis."
72. *Phil.* 4.16.

73. Kerschensteiner, "Cicero und Hirtius."
74. Decree of the Senate preserved in Macrobius *Sat.* 1.12.35 (S. Riccobono, *Fontes Juris Romani Antejustiniani,* 2nd ed. [Florence, 1968], 1, n. 42): "Whereas it is in the first month of Sextilis that the Emperor Caesar Augustus has assumed his first consulate . . . resolved that this month be called Augustus" (trans. P. V. Davies).
75. Bringmann, "Das zweite Triumvirat." Homeyer, *Die antiken Berichte über den Tod Ciceros und ihre Quellen = Helikon* 17 (1977), 56–96. In general, Hinard, *Les proscriptions de la Rome républicaine.* It seems that the exceptionally high number of coin hoards to be dated to 45–41 B.C. reflects, at least in part, the manhunts of the triumvirs (M. Crawford, *Papers of the British School at Rome* 37 [1969], 76–81, esp. 80).
76. *ad Brut.* 1.18.3. Cicero's bail: see the long climactic statement in *Phil.* 5.50–51 ending: "I give you my promise, my guarantee, my pledge, Members of the Senate, that Gaius Caesar will always be such a citizen as he is today." (1 January 43 B.C.).
77. Fragment preserved by Nonius, p. 436, 17.

Chapter Six. Epilogue

1. See, e.g., Cic. *Fam.* 6.4.2: "the consciousness of honest intentions is a sovereign consolation in adversity"; *Fin.* 3.32: "Actions springing from virtue are to be judged right from their first inception and not in their successful completion." More in K. Kumaniecki, *Philologus* 101 (1957), 113–34; Bringmann, *Untersuchungen,* 64–65. 253: "The proposition that a man's worth consists not in what he has accomplished, but rather in what he strove for, was for him, as numerous letters from the year 46 B.C. show, the real comfort in his inefficacy; it unlocked for him the door to philosophy."
2. Gelzer expresses the same view as follows: "Cicero . . . stands for a number of honest senators who, while conservative (as they wished to hold on to traditional forms of government), were not inaccessible to every reform" ("War Caesar ein Staatsmann?" 297).
3. Heinze has seen this clearly ("Ciceros *Staat* als politische Tendenzschrift," 86): "The closer one looks at Cicero's political activity in its different phases, the clearer it becomes that, from his political beginnings until his death, he remained faithful to one and the same basic persuasion."
4. Cic. *Brut.* 280 (on Curio); 273 (on Caelius).
5. *Fam.* 6.6.6, from the fall of 46 B.C.
6. Gelzer, *Cicero,* 121.
7. *Att.* 11.12.1–2.
8. *Lig.* 19.
9. *Marcell.* 29.

10. See Ungern-Sternberg, "Weltreich und Krise."
11. Hegel, *Vorlesungen zur Geschichte der Philosophie* (see below, n. 14), 311.
12. *Att.* 10.7.1.
13. *Tusc.* 1.84 (cf. 96.100). *Fam.* 9.8.2.
14. "Such are all great historical men—whose own particular aims involve those large issues which are the will of the World-Spirit" (G. W. F. Hegel, *Vorlesungen zur Geschichte der Philosophie*). These lectures were published in 1837, six years after Hegel's death. The quotation is from J. Sibree's translation (Dover Publications, 1956), 30.
15. Ibid., 311.
16. See A. Heuss, *Theodor Mommsen und das 19. Jahrhundert* (Kiel, 1956), 79; cf. 76. Girardet, *Die Ordnung der Welt,* 227–35: "Cicero, Caesar und die Reform von *res publica* und *imperium.*"
17. Gundolf, *Caesar: Geschichte seines Ruhmes,* l.c.228: "If one had nothing about Caesar besides his *Commentaries,* one would get an incomplete picture of his personality, but not a distorted one."
18. This is an expression of the fact that Gundolf's scale of values culminated in the "whole man" ("Gesamtmensch"), as observed by L. Helbing and C. V. Bock, "Friedrich Gundolf," in A. R. Evans, Jr., ed., *On Four Humanists* (Princeton, 1970), 69. And for the same reason, Gundolf also wrote monographs on Shakespeare and Goethe. The two books on Caesar have been brilliantly reviewed by M. Gelzer, *Gnomon* 2 (1926), 725–29 = *Kl.Schr.* 2 (1963), 336–40. It should be noted that in speaking of Caesar, Gundolf also has his hero George in mind.
19. Cicero often found himself under the spell of Caesar's charisma. It has been said of him: "Cicero . . . was continually tormented by the discord between Caesar's greatness and his wantonness" (Yavetz, *Julius Caesar,* 22). This seems to be inspired by Gundolf's sentence about Lord Byron: "In the appendix to *Childe Harold* he devotes a special note to Caesar's greatness and Caesar's wantonness, on that pathetic discord that first tormented Cicero" (*Caesar im neunzehnten Jahrhundert,* 17).
20. Gelzer, *Caesar. Der Politiker und Staatsmann,* first published in 1921; 6th, rev. ed., 1960, on which is based the English edition, *Caesar: Politician and Statesman,* trans. P. Needham (Cambridge, Mass., 1968). The same, *RE* Tullius (1939), 827–1091 (M. Tullius Cicero als Politiker); *Cicero. Ein biographischer Versuch.*
21. The original German text is quoted in Girardet, *Die Ordnung der Welt,* 229, n. 25.
22. *HZ* 175 (1953), 225–64.
23. *HZ* 175 (1953), 264: he stresses that the ancient tradition is completely silent on what Caesar the statesman did accomplish, silent

also on what he might have been able, and determined, to accomplish. In Strasburger's view, this silence is as suggestive as it is damaging to Caesar. Perhaps the most telling testimony is that of Gaius Matius, a close friend of Caesar. Some three weeks after Caesar's murder, he said to Cicero, with whom he had been on very good terms for some time: "if a man of Caesar's genius could find no way out, who will find one now?" (Cic. *Att.* 14.1.1).

24. Gelzer, "War Caesar ein Staatsmann?"
25. Strasburger, *Caesar im Urteil seiner Zeitgenossen,* postscript on pp. 67–81.
26. Gelzer, "War Caesar ein Staatsman?" 288: "Besides, it seemed wrong to me to withhold the title of statesman from a politician who so drastically affected the history of his country." 305: "For the events that were to come, Caesar undoubtedly led the way by pointing into the direction suitable under the circumstances. A statesman can do no better."
27. Strasburger, *Caesar im Urteil seiner Zeitgenossen,* 67: "While I still stand, in all essential points, by the contents of this research, I would now be somewhat less rigid than I was then in insisting on the absolute nature of my conclusions in the final judgment of Caesar as a statesman."
28. See, e.g., Collins, "Caesar and the Corruption of Power," 446–47; Bringmann, *Untersuchungen,* 249: "There are no indications whatsoever that he had thought, however vaguely, about a definite solution of how the Roman state might be reorganized." Meier ("Cicero," 211) observes that Caesar seemed to have been at a loss as to what to do about Rome's internal problems (221–22). A. Heuss, HZ 237 (1983), 92 ff.
29. Meier, *Caesar,* 419, writes: "The demands put forward by either side concerned Caesar's existence and that of the Republic. Legitimate as these were in themselves, they were mutually exclusive." The author seems to suggest that both were of the same order, such as demands between equal partners. That would be the case if the contest were between Caesar and Pompey. But Caesar and the Republic, as Meier correctly views the confrontation, is quite another matter. His view carries Meier to the point that he speaks of "Caesar's right to civil war" (422). All of this has been duly criticized by Heuss (preceding note), 92.
30. Gundolf (*Caesar. Geschichte seines Ruhmes*), 240, says of Goethe that he called Caesar's murder "the most senseless deed in all of history." The assassins are called "this cowardly gang" by A. Alföldi (*Studien über Caesars Monarchie* [Lund, 1953], 59), who also calls the assassination "a cowardly crime in the manner of today's gangstyle executions" (*Caesar in 44 v. Chr.,* 1.341). Contrast Syme's verdict: "They

stood not merely for the traditions and the institutions of the Free
State, but very precisely for the dignity and the interests of their own
order" (*Roman Revolution,* 59). Meyer, *Caesars Monarchie,* 530–39,
seems to do them justice.

31. M. I. Henderson, *JRS* 57 (1967), 247: "Caesar's set purpose to wreck
and to rule."

32. Plut. *Caes.* 32.5. The standard opinion that Caesar, had he abstained
from the use of force, would have been tried and condemned, mainly
based on what Asinius Pollio reported Caesar to have said at the
battlefield of Pharsalus (Suet. *Iul.* 30.4: "They would have it so. Even
I, Gaius Caesar, after so many great deeds, should have been found
guilty, if I had not turned to my army for help"), has been questioned
by Shackleton Bailey, *Cicero's Letters,* 1.38–40, and Gruen, *Last Generation,* 495 (cf. D. R. Shackleton Bailey, *AJPh* 96 [1975], 439: *"fable
convenue"*). If that is justified, it adds to the reasons why a notion such
as "Caesar's right to civil war" (Meier, *Caesar,* 422) seems to be wrong.
See, however, the objections raised by Brunt, "Cicero's *Officium* in the
Civil War," 18–19.

33. Meier, *Caesar,* 540: "His plan, therefore, is an expression of his per-
plexity towards Rome and her society." Heuss (*HZ* 237 [1983], 94):
"The monstrosity inherent in this plan . . . an escape into foreign policy." Malitz, "Caesars Partherkrieg," 58–59.

34. Admirably brought out by Smith, "The Conspiracy and the Conspirators."

35. Cass. *Dio* 47.20.4.

36. Tac. *Ann.* 3.76.1–2. Honorary mention of Brutus and Cassius interpreted as a crime: Tac. *Ann.* 4.34–35.

37. Hegel (*Vorlesungen zur Geschichte der Philosophie,* 312): "But it was not
the mere accident of Caesar's existence that destroyed the Republic—
it was *Necessity.*"

38. Ibid., 314: "the noblest men of Rome . . . Cicero, Brutus, and Cassius
. . . . Brutus, a man of highly noble character . . . ." On Brutus, the
fine psychological study of Seel, *Cicero: Wort, Staat, Welt,* 417–43, is
well worth reading. Strasburger, *Caesar,* 71, judges: "it is certainly
unjustified for historians to hold the assassins alone accountable for
the premature end of Caesar's rule, instead of Caesar himself."

39. See most recently Girardet, *Die Ordnung der Welt,* 227–35.

40. *Fam.* 1.9.7, from the end of 54 B.C., with the comments of Meyer,
Caesars Monarchie, 135, n. 1.

41. It was only during the last stage of his fight against Antonius that
Cicero went beyond his usual self, by suggesting to Brutus that he
execute his prisoner Gaius Antonius (*ad Brut.* 1.2a.2; 3.3; 3a; cf.
1.4.2) and when he moved that punitive measures against Lepidus
for treason should be extended to Lepidus's children (*ad Brut.*

1.15.10–11; 13; cf. 1.13.1). He realized that he might be accused of cruelty, but said that clemency could result in the defeat of the cause. At Brutus's request, however, he spared Lepidus's children (their mother was Brutus's sister). Brutus long spared Gaius Antonius, whose fate he wished to have decided by the Senate or the people, but eventually had him executed after he learned that Cicero had been slain.

42. See, e.g., Smith, *Cicero*, 62.

43. See Rawson, *Cicero*, 159: "Whatever the shortcomings of Cicero's political works, there is no evidence that any of his contemporaries understood the problems of the time as clearly or indeed produced nearly so positive a contribution towards solving them as he did." She goes on to explain that she had, among others, Cato, Caesar, and Sallust in mind.

44. *Brut.* 330: "I have indeed reason to grieve that I entered on the road of life so late that the night, which has fallen upon the commonwealth, has overtaken me before my journey was ended."

45. Stockton, *Cicero*, 306, echoing Cicero's own statement (preceding note).

46. Ibid. 245.

47. "Cicero's finest hour" (P. A. Brunt, *CR* 81 [1967], 346); "the heroic period of Cicero's career" (Rawson, *Cicero*, 278); "perhaps the most glorious, certainly the most courageous period of his life" (Smith, *Cicero*, 244); "turn to courage and energy, the real summit of his political career" (A. Heuss, *Römische Geschichte* [Braunschweig, 1960], 218). Shackleton Bailey, *Cicero*, 34.

48. *Phil.* 3.12: "In barring him from Gaul . . . Brutus judges that he is no consul, and he is entirely right. Accordingly, Members of the Senate, it is our duty to approve Decimus Brutus's initiative by public authority."

49. *Phil.* 2.113. *Velleius* 2.62.3: "Brutus and Cassius . . . without government sanction . . . had taken possession of provinces and armies, and under the pretense that the republic existed wherever they were . . . ."

50. *Phil.* 11.27. See Bleicken's note, *Lex publica*, 504, n. 437.

51. *Phil.* 11.28.

52. Cic. *Phil.* 10.12, where he has C. Antonius in mind; *Phil.* 13.14, where Lepidus is the target. Such a doctrine is about as convincing as Cicero's point that a citizen who commits hostile acts against the state thereby automatically loses his citizenship (Chap. 3 above), an argument to which even M. Brutus was strongly opposed (Chap. 3 above, n. 12).

53. Smith, *Cicero*, 258. See, however, Bleicken, "Der Begriff der Freiheit in der letzten Phase der römischen Republik," who points out that republican freedom at the time had already been narrowed to mean

aristocratic freedom. Similarly, Wirszubski, *Libertas as a Political Idea at Rome*, 95: "gradually the conviction struck root that what was offered under the name of libertas was not worth fighting and dying for."

54. *Res gestae* 34.1: "I transferred the republic from my own control to the will of the senate and the Roman people." I subscribe to the general interpretation of these words in modern studies, despite the vigorous attack against it by E. A. Judge, "*Res Publica Restituta*, A Modern Illusion?," *Polis and Imperium, Studies in Honour of Edward Togo Salmon* (Toronto, 1974), 279–311. See also Ch. Meier, "Augustus. Die Begründung der Monarchie als Wiederherstellung der Republik," in Meier, *Ohnmacht*, 223–87.

55. Bellen, "Cicero und der Aufstieg Octavians," 189. In an unpublished paper on "Augustus und die Macht der Tradition" (which he kindly allowed me to see and to quote), W. Eder argues that Augustus's claim to have restored the Republic was closer to the truth than is commonly believed. He too credits mainly Cicero for that.

56. Earlier opinions are discussed by K. Wickert, *RE* Princeps (1954), 2227–29, more recent ones in H. Cambeis, "Das monarchische Element und die Funktion der Magistrate in Ciceros Verfassungsentwurf," *Gymnasium* 91 (1984), 237–60, on pp. 258–60. See especially Schäfer, "Cicero und der Prinzipat des Augustus." Too skeptical, it seems to me, is the view of Syme (*Roman Revolution*, 321): "Only a robust faith can discover authentic relics of Cicero in the Republic of Augustus," with reference to Wilamowitz, *Der Glaube der Hellenen* 2 (Berlin, 1932), 428, note 1.

57. See, e.g., Alföldi, *Oktavians Aufstieg zur Macht*, 125, where he says that Augustus tolerated "a republican romantic" and continues: "With it, the intellectual heritage of another great murder victim acquired full currency, Cicero's work of a lifetime. His political conception of Rome, the moral foundations of his political thinking, the humanity grounded in philosophy he had learned from the Greeks, all this became common property and formed the ethical backbone of imperial Rome."

58. Fuhrmann, "Cum dignitate otium," 490, n. 27.

59. Cic. *Phil.* 1.38; cf. *Marc.* 25. The connection has been observed also by Alföldi, *Caesar in 44 v. Chr.*, 1.285, n. 727.

60. A. Heuss, *Rom. Die römische Welt*, Propyläen-Weltgeschichte, eds. G. Mann and A. Heuss (Berlin, 1963), 4.248.

Select Bibliography

Abel, K. "Zu Caesars *Anticato*." *MH* 18 (1961), 230–31.

Alföldi, A. *Oktavians Aufstieg zur Macht.* Bonn, 1976.

—————. *Caesar in 44 v. Chr., 1, Studien zu Caesars Monarchie und ihren Wurzeln.* Edited from his papers by H. Wolff, E. Alföldi-Rosenbaum, and G. Stumpf. Bonn, 1985.

Allen, W. J., Jr. "Caesar's *Regnum* (Suet. *Iul.* 9.2)." *TAPA* 84 (1953), 227–36.

Astbury, R. "Varro and Pompey." *CQ* 17 (1967), 403–7.

Astin, A. E. "Cicero and the Censorship." *CP* 80 (1985), 233–39.

Badian, E. *Publicans and Sinners.* Ithaca, N.Y., 1972.

Balsdon, J. P. V. D. "Roman History 58–56 B.C.: Three Ciceronian Problems." *JRS* 47 (1957), 15–20.

—————. "Roman history 65–50 B.C.: Five Problems." *JRS* 52 (1962), 134–41.

—————. "*Fabula Clodiana.*" *Historia* 15 (1966), 65–73.

Becker, C. "Cicero." *RAC* 3 (1957), 86–127.

Bellen, H. "Cicero und der Aufstieg Octavians." *Gymnasium* 92 (1985), 161–89.

Bellincioni, C. H. *Cicerone politico nel' ultimo anno di vita.* Brescia, 1974.

Benario, H. W. "*Cicero, rei publicae amantissimus.*" *CJ* 69 (1973), 12–20.

Bengtson, H. "Die letzten Monate der römischen Senatsherrschaft." *ANRW* 1.1 (1972), 967–81.

Benner, H. *Die Politik des P. Clodius Pulcher.* Stuttgart, 1987.

Béranger, J. "Dans la tempête: Cicéron entre Pompée et César (50–44 av. J.-C.)." In Béranger, *Principatus*, 107–15.

————. "Cicéron précurseur politique." In Béranger, *Principatus*, 117–34.

————. *Principatus*. Geneva, 1973.

Bleicken, J. "Der Begriff der Freiheit in der letzten Phase der römischen Republik." *HZ* 195 (1962), 1–20.

————. *Lex publica. Gesetz und Recht in der römischen Republik*. Berlin, 1975.

Borzsák, St. "Cicero und Caesar. Ihre Beziehungen im Spiegel des Romulus-Mythos." In *Ciceroniana. Hommages à Kazimierz Kumaniecki*, 22–35. Leiden, 1975.

Boyancé, P. "Cicéron et Athènes." *Epistemonike Epeteris Athenon* 24 (1973–74), 156–69.

Braunert, H. "Zum Eingangssatz der *res gestae Divi Augusti*." *Chiron* 4 (1974), 343–58.

Bringmann, K. *Untersuchungen zum späten Cicero*. Göttingen, 1971.

————. "Das Enddatum der gallischen Statthalterschaft Caesars." *Chiron* 8 (1978), 345–56.

————. "Der Diktator Caesar als Richter? Zu Ciceros Reden 'Pro Ligario' und 'Pro rege Deiotaro.'" *Hermes* 114 (1986), 72–88.

————. "Das zweite Triumvirat. Bemerkungen zu Mommsens Lehre von der ausserordentlichen konstituierenden Gewalt." *Alte Geschichte und Wissenschaftsgeschichte*. Festschrift Karl Christ, 22–38. Darmstadt, 1988.

Broughton, T. R. S. *The Magistrates of the Roman Republic*. 3 vols. New York, 1952 (vols. 1–2); Atlanta, 1986 (vol. 3).

Brunt, P. A. "The Role of the Senate in the Augustan Regime." *CQ* 78 (1984), 423–44.

————. "Cicero's *Officium* in the Civil War." *JRS* 76 (1986), 12–32.

Büchner, K. *Cicero. Bestand und Wandel seiner geistigen Welt*. Heidelberg, 1964.

Cavarzaro, A. *Marco Celio Rufo, Lettere*. (Cic. *Fam.* 1.VIII). Testo, apparato critico, introduzione, versione e commento. Brescia, 1983.

Christopherson, A. J. "Invidia Ciceronis: Some Political Circumstances Involving Cicero's Exile and Return." Festschrift W. Jashemski (forthcoming).

Ciaceri, E. *Cicerone e i suoi tempi*. 2 vols. Milan, Rome, Naples, 1926–30.

Cipriani, G. "La *Pro Marcello* e il suo significato come orazione politica." *A & R* 22 (1977), 213–25.

Classen, C. J. "Cicero, the Laws and the Law-Courts." *Latomus* 37 (1978), 597–619.

Collins, J. H. "Caesar and the Corruption of Power." *Historia* 4 (1955), 445–65. Trans. "Caesar und die Verführung der Macht," in D. Rasmussen, ed., *Caesar*, 379–412. Darmstadt, 1967.

Crawford, J. W. M. *Tullius Cicero: The Lost and Unpublished Orations.* Göttingen, 1984.

Crook, J. A. "Was There a 'Doctrine of Manifest Guilt' in the Roman Criminal Law?" *PCPS* 213 (1987), 38–52.

Dahlmann, H. "Cicero, Caesar und der Untergang der libera res publica." *Gymnasium* 75 (1968), 337–55.

Deroux, C. "L'identité de Lesbie." *ANRW* 1.3 (1973), 390–416.

Dorey, T. A., ed. *Cicero.* New York, 1965.

Drumann, W. K. A. *Geschichte Roms in seinem Uebergange von der republicanischen zur monarchischen Verfassung oder Pompejus, Caesar, Cicero und ihre Zeitgenossen nach Geschlechtern und genealogischen Tabellen.* 6 vols. Königsberg, 1834–44.

Eder, W. "Augustus und die Macht der Tradition." (forthcoming).

Epstein, D. F. "Cicero's Testimony at the *bona-Dea* Trial." *CP* 81 (1986), 229–35.

Fantham, E. "The Trials of Gabinius in 54 B.C." *Historia* 24 (1975), 425–43.

Ferguson, J. "Some Ancient Judgments of Cicero." In E. Paratore, ed., *Collana di studi Ciceroniani* 2 (Rome, 1962), 9–33.

Frier, B. "Cicero's Management of Urban Properties." *CJ* 74 (1978), 1–6.

Frisch, H. *Cicero's Fight for the Republic. The Historical Background of Cicero's Philippics.* Copenhagen, 1946.

Fuhrmann, M. "Cum dignitate otium. Politisches Programm und Staatstheorie bei Cicero." *Gymnasium* 67 (1960), 481–500.

Gabba, E. "Cicerone e la falsificazione dei senatoconsulti." *StudClassOrient* 10 (1961), 89–96.

——————. "Per un'interpretazione politica del *De officiis* di Cicerone." *Rendic.Accad.Lincei* 34 (1979), 117–41.

Gelzer, M. *Cicero. Ein biographischer Versuch.* Wiesbaden, 1969.

——————. *Die Nobilität der römischen Republik.* Leipzig-Berlin, 1912.

——————. *Cicero und Caesar.* Wiesbaden, 1968.

——————. "War Caesar ein Staatsmann?" *HZ* 178 (1954), 449–70 (*Kl.Schr.* 2 [1963], 286–306).

——————. Review of Gundolf, *Caesar. Geschichte seines Ruhmes,* and Gundolf, *Caesar im neunzehnten Jahrhundert. Gnomon* 2 (1926), 725–29.

Giannelli, C. A. "Le date di scadenza dei proconsolati di Giulio Cesare." *AnnPisa* 35 (1966), 107–20.

Gilboa, A. "The Dating of the Cicero-Matius Correspondence (*Fam.* 11.27–28)." *Historia* 23 (1974), 217–28.

Giovannini, A. *Consulare Imperium.* Basel, 1983.

Girardet, K. M. *Die Ordnung der Welt. Ein Beitrag zur philosophischen und politischen Interpretation von Ciceros Schrift De legibus.* Wiesbaden, 1983.

————. "Die Lex Iulia de provinciis. Vorgeschichte, Inhalt, Wirkungen." *RhM* 130 (1987), 291–329.

Glucker, J. "As Has Been Rightly Said—by Me." *LCM* 13 (1988), 6–9.

Gottlieb, G. "Zur Chronologie in Caesars erstem Konsulat." *Chiron* 4 (1974), 243–50.

Graff, J. *Ciceros Selbstauffassung.* Heidelberg, 1963.

Grasmueck, E. "Ciceros Verbannung aus Rom. Analyse eines politischen Details." *Bonner Festgabe Johannes Straub,* 165–77. Bonn, 1977.

Green, P. "Imperial Caesar." In Green, *Essays in Antiquity,* 96–108. Cleveland and New York, 1960.

Griffin, M. "Philosophy, Cato, and Roman Suicide." *G & R* 33 (1986), 64–77, 192–202.

Grimal, P. *Études de chronologie Cicéronienne (années 58 et 57 av. J.-C.).* Paris, 1967.

Gruen, E. *The Last Generation of the Roman Republic.* Berkeley, 1974.

Gundolf, F. *Caesar. Geschichte seines Ruhmes.* Berlin, 1925.

————. *Caesar im neunzehnten Jahrhundert.* Berlin, 1926.

Heinze, R. "Ciceros politische Anfänge." *Abh. Leipzig* 27 (1909), 947–1010. Reprinted in Heinze, *Vom Geist des Römertums,* 3rd ed., 87–140. Stuttgart, 1960.

————. "Ciceros *Staat* als politische Tendenzschrift." *Hermes* 59 (1924), 73–94.

Heldmann, K. "Ciceros Laelius und die Grenzen der Freundschaft." *Hermes* 104 (1976), 72–103.

Heuss, A. "Ciceros Theorie vom römischen Staat." *NAG,* no. 8 (1975), 195–272.

————. "Cicero und Matius. Zur Psychologie der revolutionären Situation in Rom." *Historia* 5 (1956), 53–73.

————. "Matius als Zeuge von Caesars staatsmännischer Grösse." *Historia* 11 (1962), 118–22.

Hinard, F. "Le *Pro Quinctio,* un discours politique?" *REA* 77 (1975), 88–107.

————. *Les proscriptions de la Rome républicaine.* Rome, 1985.

Holleman, A. W. J. "Cicero's Reaction to the Julian Calendar (Plut. *Caes.* 59); January 4th (45)." *Historia* 27 (1978), 496–98.

Homeyer, H. *Die antiken Berichte über den Tod Ciceros und ihre Quellen.* Baden-Baden, 1964.

Jackson, St. "M. Caelius Rufus." *Hermathena* 126 (1979), 55–67.

Jal, P. "Hostis (publicus) dans la littérature latine de la fin de la république." *REA* 65 (1963), 53–79.

Jones, C. P. "Cicero's *Cato.*" *RhM* 113 (1970), 188–96.

Kerschensteiner, J. "Cicero und Hirtius." *Studien zur Alten Geschichte Siegfried Lauffer dargebracht,* 2.559–75. Rome, 1986.

Kierdorf, W. "Ciceros *Cato.*" *RhM* 121 (1978), 167–84.

Kinsey, T. E. "The Political Insignificance of Cicero's *Pro Roscio.*" *LCM* 7 (1982), 39–40.

————. "The Case against Sextus Roscius of Ameria." *Antcl.* 54 (1985), 188–96.

Klingner, F. "Cicero." In Klingner, *Römische Geisteswelt,* 4th ed., 110–59. Munich, 1961.

Knight, D. W. "The Political Acumen of Cicero after the Death of Caesar." *Latomus* 27 (1968), 157–64.

Kumaniecki, K. "Ciceros *Cato.*" *Forschungen zur römischen Literatur* Festschrift K. Büchner, 168–88. Wiesbaden, 1970.

————. "Cicero: Mensch, Politiker, Schriftsteller." In K. Büchner, ed., *Das neue Cicerobild,* 348–70. Darmstadt, 1971.

————. *Cicerone e la crisi della repubblica Romana.* In E. Paratore, ed., *Collana di studi Ciceroniani* 5 (Rome, 1972).

Kytzler, B. "Matius and Cicero." *Historia* 9 (1960), 96–121.

————. "Beobachtungen zu den Matiusbriefen (Ad fam. XI 27–28)." *Philologus* 104 (1960), 48–62.

Lacey, W. K. "Clodius and Cicero, a question of dignitas." *Antichthon* 8 (1974), 85–92.

Lehmann, G. A. *Politische Reformvorschläge in der Krise der späten römischen Republik.* Meisenheim, 1980.

Lendle, O. "Ciceros ὑπόμνημα περὶ τῆς ὑπατείας." *Hermes* 95 (1967), 90–107.

Lepage, Y. G. "Cicéron avant la mort de Tullia, d'après sa correspondance." *Etcl.* 44 (1976), 245–58.

Linderski, J. "Three Trials in 54 B.C.: Sufenas, Cato, Procilius and Cicero 'ad Atticum' 4.15.4." *Studi Volterra* 2 (Milano, 1971), 281–302.

————. "Rome, Aphrodisias and the *Res Gestae: The Genera Militiae* and the Status of Octavian." *JRS* 74 (1984), 74–80.

Lintott, A. W. *Violence in Republican Rome.* Oxford, 1968.

————. "Cicero and Milo." *JRS* 64 (1974), 62–78.

McDermott, W. C. "Cicero's Publication of His Consular Orations." *Philologus* 116 (1972), 277–84.

Malitz, J. "Caesars Partherkrieg." *Historia* 33 (1984), 21–59.

————. "Die Kanzlei Caesars—Herrschaftsorganisation zwischen Republik und Prinzipat." *Historia* 26 (1987), 51–72.

Mandel, J. "Complementary Addenda to the Cicero-Matius Correspondence." *Athenaeum* 59 (1981), 191–95.

Martin, P. "Cicéron Princeps." *Latomus* 29 (1980), 850–78.

Meier, Ch. *Res publica amissa.* Wiesbaden, 1966.

————. "Ciceros Consulat." In G. Radke, ed., *Cicero, ein Mensch seiner Zeit,* 61–116. Berlin, 1968.

————. "Caesars Bürgerkrieg." In Meier, *Entstehung des Begriffs Demokratie,* 70–150. Frankfurt, 1970.

————. "Cicero. Das erfolgreiche Scheitern des Neulings in der alten Republik." In Meier, *Ohnmacht*, 101–222.

————. *Caesar*. Berlin, 1982.

————. "Die Ersten unter den Ersten des Senats." In *Gedächtsnisschrift für W. Kunkel*, 185–204. Frankfurt/Main, 1984.

————. *Die Ohnmacht des allmächtigen Dictators Caesar*. Frankfurt, 1980.

Metaxaki-Mitrou, F. "Violence in the *Contio* during the Ciceronian Age." *Antcl.* 54 (1985), 180–87.

Meyer, Ed. *Caesars Monarchie und das Principat des Pompeius*. 3rd ed. Stuttgart and Berlin, 1922.

Mitchell, Th. N. *Cicero: The Ascending Years*. New Haven, 1979.

Mittelstadt, M. C. "Cicero's Political *Velificatio Mutata:* 54 B.C.–51 B.C.: Compromise or capitulation?" *PP* 40 (1985), 13–28.

Moreau, Ph. "Cicéron, Clodius et la publication de *pro Murena*." *REL* 58 (1980), 220–37.

————. *Clodiana Religio: Un procès politique en 61 av. J.-C.* Paris, 1982.

————. "La lex Clodia sur le bannissement de Cicéron." *Athenaeum* 75 (1987), 465–92.

Nicolet, C. "Arpinum, Aemilius Scaurus et les Tullii Cicerones." *REL* 45 (1967), 276–304.

Oltramare, A. "La réaction Cicéronienne et les débuts du Principat." *REL* 10 (1932), 58–90.

Parrish, E. J. "The Senate on January 1, 62 B.C.." *CW* 65 (1972), 160–68.

Payre, M. "*Homo novus:* un slogan de Caton à César?" *Historia* 30 (1981), 22–81.

Phillips, J. J. "Atticus and the Publication of Cicero's Works." *CW* 79 (1986), 227–37.

Pöschl, V. "Quelques principes fondamentaux de la politique de Cicéron." *CRAI* (1987), 340–50.

Raaflaub, K. *Dignitatis Contentio. Studien zur Motivation und politischen Taktik im Bürgerkrieg zwischen Pompeius und Caesar*. München, 1974.

Radke, G., ed. *Cicero, ein Mensch seiner Zeit*. Berlin, 1968.

Raskolnikoff, M. "La richesse et les riches chez Cicéron." *Ktema* 2 (1977), 357–72.

Raubitschek, A. E. "Phaidros and His Roman Pupils." *Hesperia* 18 (1949), 96–103.

————. "Brutus in Athens." *Phoenix* 11 (1957), 1–11.

Rauh, N. R. "Cicero's Business Friendships: Economics and Politics in the Late Roman Republic." *Aevum* 80 (1986), 3–30.

Rawson, E. "Lucius Crassus and Cicero: The Formation of a Statesman?" *PCPS* 197 (1971), 75–88.

————. *Cicero. A Portrait*. London, 1975.

————. "Cicero and the Areopagus." *Athenaeum* 73 (1985), 44–67.

Rolin, G. "La jeunesse perturbée de M. Tullius Cicéron." *Etcl.* 47 (1979), 335–46; 48 (1980), 43–61.

Rossi, R. F. "Bruto, Cicerone e la congiura contro Cesare." *PP* 8 (1953), 26–47.

Rowland, R. J. "The Origins and Developments of Cicero's Friendship with Pompey." *Riv. stor. ant.* 6–7 (1976–77), 329–41.

Ruebel, J. S. "When Did Cicero Learn about the Conference at Luca?" *Historia* 24 (1975), 622–24.

————. "The Trial of Milo in 52 B.C.: A Chronological Study." *TAPA* 109 (1979), 231–49.

Rundell, W. "Cicero and Clodius: The Question of Credibility." *Historia* 28 (1979), 301–28.

Schäfer, M. "Cicero und der Prinzipat des Augustus." *Gymnasium* 64 (1957), 310–35.

Schickel, A. "Gedanken über wirtschaftliche und soziale Fragen in Ciceros Konsulatsreden." In *Studien zur Alten Geschichte Siegfried Lauffer dargebracht*, 805–34. Rome, 1986.

Schmidt, P. L. "Cicero *De re publica*. Die Forschung der letzten fünf Dezennien." *ANRW* 1.4 (1973), 262–333.

Schwartz, E. "Cicero." In Schwartz, *Charakterköpfe aus der Antike*, 2nd ed., 95–115. Leipzig, 1943.

Seager, R. "*Iusta Catilinae*." *Historia* 21 (1973), 240–48.

————. "Clodius, Pompeius and the Exile of Cicero." *Latomus* 24 (1965), 519–31.

Seel, O. *Cicero: Wort, Staat, Welt*. Stuttgart, 1953. (3rd ed., 1967).

Setaioli, A. "On the Date of Publication of *Cicero's Letters to Atticus*." *SymbOsl* 51 (1976), 105–20.

Shackleton Bailey, D. R. *Cicero*. London, 1971.

————. *Cicero's Letters to Atticus*. 7 vols. Cambridge, 1965–70.

Shatzman, I. *Senatorial Wealth and Roman Politics*. Brussels, 1975.

Simélon, P. "A propos des émeutes de M. Caelius Rufus et de P. Cornelius Dolabella (48–47 av. J.-C.)." *Etcl.* 53 (1985), 338–405.

Sirianni, F. A. "Caesar's Decision to Cross the Rubicon." *Antcl.* 48 (1979), 636–38.

Smith, R. E. *Cicero the Statesman*. Cambridge, Eng., 1966.

————. "The Conspiracy and the Conspirators." *G & R* 26 (1957), 58–70.

Stockton, D. *Cicero. A Political Biography*. Oxford, 1971.

————. "*Quis iustius induit arma?*" *Historia* 24 (1975), 232–59.

Stone, A. M. "*Pro Milone*, Cicero's Second Thoughts." *Antichthon* 14 (1980), 88–111.

Strasburger, H. "Novus homo." *RE* 17 (1936), 1223–38.

————. *Caesar im Urteil seiner Zeitgenossen.* 2nd ed. Darmstadt, 1968. (Also in Strasburger, *Studien zur Alten Geschichte* 1 [Hildesheim, 1982], 343–421).

Stroh, W. *Taxis und Taktik. Die advokatische Dispositionskunst in Ciceros Gerichtsreden.* Stuttgart, 1975.

————. "Ciceros demosthenische Redezyklen." *MH* 40 (1983), 35–50.

————. "Die Provinzverlosung am 28. November 44." *Hermes* 111 (1983), 452–58.

Syme, R. *The Roman Revolution.* Oxford, 1939.

Thompson, L. H. "Cicero the Politician." In E. Paratore, ed., *Collana di Studi Ciceroniani* 2 (Rome, 1962), 9–33.

Townend, G. B. "A Clue to Caesar's Unfulfilled Intentions." *Latomus* 42 (1983), 601–6.

Tschiedel, H. J. *Caesars 'Anticato.'* Darmstadt, 1981 (Impulse der Forschung).

Twyman, B. L. "The Date of Sulla's Abdication and the Chronology of the First Book of Appian's *Civil Wars.*" *Athenaeum* 64 (1976), 77–97.

Tyrrell, R. Y., and Purser, L. C., eds. *The Correspondence of M. Tullius Cicero.* 6 vols. 2nd and 3rd eds. Dublin and London, 1904–33.

Tyrrell, W. B. *A Legal and Historical Commentary to Cicero's Oratio pro C. Rabirio perduellionis reo.* Amsterdam, 1978.

Ungern-Sternberg, J. von. *Untersuchungen zum spätrepublikanischen Notstandsrecht.* Munich, 1970.

————. "Weltreich und Krise: Äussere Bedingungen für den Niedergang der römischen Republik." *MH* 39 (1982), 254–71.

Vanderbroeck, P. "*Homo novus* again." *Chiron* 16 (1986), 293–42.

Vogt, J. *Homo novus.* Stuttgart, 1926.

Ward, A. M. "The Conference of Luca: Did It Happen?" *AJAH* 5 (1980), 48–63.

Wieacker, F. *Cicero als Advokat.* Berlin, 1965.

Wirszubski, Ch. *Libertas as a Political Idea at Rome during the Late Republic and Early Principate.* Cambridge, Eng., 1960.

Wiseman, T. P. *New Men in the Roman Senate 139 B.C.–A.D. 14.* Oxford, 1971.

Wistrand, M. *Cicero Imperator. Studies in Cicero's Correspondence 51–47 B.C..* Göteborg, 1979.

Wood, N. *Cicero's Social and Political Thought.* Berkeley, 1988.

Yavetz, Z. *Julius Caesar and His Public Image.* Ithaca, N.Y., 1983.

Zecchini, G. "La morte di Catone e l'opposizione intellettuale a Cesare e ad Augusto." *Athenaeum* 68 (1980), 39–56.

Zielinski, Th. *Cicero im Wandel der Jahrhunderte.* 4th ed. Leipzig and Berlin, 1929.

Index

ANCIENT SOCIETY AND HISTORY

The series Ancient Society and History offers books, relatively brief in compass, on selected topics in the history of ancient Greece and Rome, broadly conceived, with a special emphasis on comparative and other nontraditional approaches and methods. The series, which includes both works of synthesis and works of original scholarship, is aimed at the widest possible range of specialist and nonspecialist readers.

Published in the series:
Eva Cantarella, PANDORA'S DAUGHTERS: The Role and
    Status of Women in Greek and Roman Antiquity, translated by
    Maureen B. Fant
Alan Watson, ROMAN SLAVE LAW
John E. Stambaugh, THE ANCIENT ROMAN CITY
Géza Alfödy, THE SOCIAL HISTORY OF ROME, trans-
    lated by David Braund and Frank Pollock
Giovanni Comotti, MUSIC IN GREEK AND ROMAN
    CULTURE,
Christian Habicht, CICERO THE POLITICIAN